The Camper's Guide to
ALASKA, THE YUKON,
AND NORTHERN
BRITISH COLUMBIA

Books by Raymond Bridge

America's Backpacking Book

The Complete Snow Camper's Guide

Climbing: A Guide to Mountaineering

The Camper's Guide to Alaska, the Yukon,
and Northern British Columbia

The Camper's Guide to
ALASKA, THE YUKON,
AND NORTHERN
BRITISH COLUMBIA

by Raymond Bridge

Published by CHARLES SCRIBNER'S SONS · New York

To Maddie,
for reasons too numerous
to list

1 3 5 7 9 11 13 15 17 19 c/c 20 18 16 14 12 10 8 6 4 2
1 3 5 7 9 11 13 15 17 19 c/p 20 18 16 14 12 10 8 6 4 2

Printed in the United States of America
Library of Congress Catalog Card Number 75-42587
ISBN 0-684-14393-3 (cloth)
ISBN 0-684-14394-1 (paper)

Contents

Introduction

Alaska! The Yukon! The names alone conjure up excitement for many Americans. Though most of us know little of this country, we have heard stories from gold rush times, have read about Eskimos and northern Indian tribes, or have had our imaginations stirred by tales of mountaineering, exploration, canoe trips, and other adventures in the North. Whether one is drawn by interest in its unique wildlife or by the thought of great stands of forest, unexplored mountain ranges, and vast regions of arctic tundra, the North holds a special fascination for the camper and for all those who love the outdoors.

The North makes up the last great wilderness on this continent. There is no longer anything to compare with it south of the border between Canada and the United States. This great wilderness stretches across the North American continent, but it reaches its climax in the Northwest, where the great chains of the western mountains stretch into an immense and nearly roadless country.

This book was written to help visitors from the more populous parts of the United States and Canada to explore Alaska, the Yukon, and the northern part of the Province of British Columbia. These three political divisions, together with parts of the Northwest Territories, make up a logical whole. To drive to Alaska, for example, one must first go through northern British Columbia and then the Yukon. The Marine Highway to Alaska, the system of ferries run by the state of Alaska, ends at Haines, and to drive to Anchorage or

1

Fairbanks, the two major Alaskan cities, one must go through the southwestern corner of the Yukon. Thus, unless one travels by air, a camping trip to Alaska inevitably means a camping trip in northwestern Canada as well.

Living out-of-doors is the best way to explore this country. Even close to the roads, most of it is still untouched by man, so its attractions are not those of civilization but those of nature, and the visitor who lives in the open as much as possible will be best able to appreciate the North, the last great wilderness on this continent.

Alaska and the Canadian Northwest

For the traveler planning a first trip to the northern wilderness of the American hemisphere, the first difficulty that must be surmounted is that of getting a feeling for the size and immensity of the region. Few of us have had any experience to guide us in realizing just how big Alaska, or the Yukon, or northern British Columbia, is. In addition to our lack of firsthand knowledge, we have gotten used to many maps that are projected in such a way as to shrink the northern regions by comparison with the more urbanized areas to the south.

Dozens of statistical illustrations can be given, all of them deficient in conveying any true feeling for the vastness of the country. Alaska, the Yukon, and northern British Columbia are over a third the size of all the forty-eight contiguous states.

From a practical point of view, the main consequence of the great distances of the North country is that any attempt to "do" or "see" all of Alaska, or the Yukon, or British Columbia, is silly. One can see only a small part, and it is

Glaciers come right to the road at many places in Alaska and elsewhere in the North.

usually a waste of time to rush around in an attempt to squeeze more miles into the trip. The most successful visits are likely to be those that concentrate on one or several specific areas. Even a small part of this huge domain would require a lifetime for thorough exploration.

The Seasons

The far North is, of course, the "land of the midnight sun," though the terminology is only really accurate in the lands north of the Arctic Circle, perhaps a third of Alaska, and a smaller part of the Yukon. Still, in late spring and early summer, daylight lasts nearly around the clock in much of the

North. Many people seem to need less sleep in these circumstances, and one is always surprised to find that it is far later than expected.

In winter months, the process is reversed, and for some people as well as animals, this is a time of hibernation. Except for the hardiest, it is not a time for camping, and little information is included in this book on camping in the winter months. Anyone competent to stay outdoors in the North country during the winter will know enough already and will require no additional information.

Spring, summer, and fall are the times when most visitors are likely to spend time camping in the North. Though summer is the most popular season, spring and fall are very pleasant, providing one is adequately prepared for the less predictable weather. Spring comes later to the North country, so snows and cold snaps can be expected at later dates, and roads muddy from spring thaw may persist well into June. The sparkling spring days are incomparable, however, if one is equipped for them.

July and August are the real summer months in the North. Temperatures can be warm, though it is usually the long hours of sunlight that make them seem hotter than they really are. Mosquitos and other insects linger on through the summer and, except during rainy periods, dust is likely to be more of a problem on roads than mud.

Fall days are shorter and chillier, but frosts virtually eliminate bugs, autumn colors beguile the eye, and crowds have gone. The tundra has usually dried out and this makes for easy walking during the fall in spots that are difficult to reach earlier. The great caribou migrations present an awesome sight. As with other parts of the continent, fall reaches different sections of the North at different times, and one can often follow the colors from north to south or from inland toward the coast.

Weather and Climate

The weather and climate in Alaska, the Yukon, and northern British Columbia vary tremendously, though this fact is not surprising when one considers the vast area and range of latitudes. The north-south range from Prince Rupert, British Columbia (on the coast near the southern tip of Alaska), to Barrow, Alaska (on the North Slope), is roughly the same as that from the Mexican border to Canada. The range of climatic conditions is different in the North, but it is just as great as that between the area extending from Death Valley in California to the Olympic Peninsula in Washington.

The coastal regions of Alaska and British Columbia, particularly those southeast of the Alaska Peninsula and the Aleutian Islands, tend to have a moderate, wet climate. Heavy rains and sea breezes keep the coast cool in summer, and the sea moderates the winter chill. Winter lows along the southeastern Alaska coast are less severe than those of Montana or the Dakotas. Precipitation is another matter. Annual rain and snowfall along the coast are very high everywhere, and in some sections it is phenomenal, with clear days practically nonexistent.

As one moves farther inland, one finds colder winters, warmer summers, and generally drier weather. In some inland areas rainfall is so low that the climate might be considered arid. Though temperatures in such regions can stay under $-50°$ F. for weeks at a time in winter, in summer they can be quite warm.

Moving to a higher altitude has the same effect as going north, and when a hiker is already in subarctic regions, going up a few thousand feet can take him or her from dense coniferous forest into a zone of perpetual snow. This fact, combined with the extremely heavy precipitation along the

Spectacular scenery like this is common along many of the winding gravel roads of the North.

coast, results in very heavy glaciation in many of the mountainous areas of the north. Huge active glaciers are the sources for many northern rivers, a fact that accounts for the quantities of silt in many streams and lakes. Many glaciers drop all the way to the sea. The non-mountaineering tourist can see large glaciers at close range from the deck of a boat or the seat of a car.

The Country

Though many tourist attractions of the more conventional type can be found in the North, its primary attraction is the vast wilderness to be found a short distance off the main roads. Despite rapid development and depredation, there are tremendous areas that are still a haven for wildlife and for those who love unspoiled country. Whether your particular dream is of peaceful weeks beside a remote lake, watching the trout jump, a backpacking trip through country with little or no sign of human disturbance, or a first ascent of an isolated peak, the prospects awaiting you are limitless. There are mountain massifs as large as any in the world, great expanses of arctic tundra, almost impenetrable rain forest, and wilderness lakes, streams, and inlets beyond counting.

The difficulties of generalizing about such a large and varied country should be obvious. The contrasts between the inland lake country of British Columbia, the precipitous forests along the coast, the forbidding shores of the Aleutians, the tundra slopes north of the Brooks Range, and the great river deltas are overpowering. The common bond is the sheer size of the region.

Great as the North country is, man is beginning to make his mark, and it is often an ugly one. Much of the North is surprisingly fragile, with long winters and difficult climatic conditions making the existence of life a tenuous thing. Respect for the processes of nature is more important here than in temperate zones, and the visitor should learn to tread lightly.

How to Use This Book

The first few chapters discuss the various ways of traveling to Alaska: highways, ferries, air, and so forth. Maps are included in each section to show all the public campgrounds along the way, together with keys giving information about each one. Chapter 1—Driving to Alaska—includes maps of the Alaska Highway showing campgrounds, and facing each map is a key to the campgrounds shown. This chapter also includes general information on driving in the North, the possible routes, camping along the new Coast Range Highway, and so forth.

Similarly, detailed information on campgrounds around the coastal towns along the Marine Highway, the ferry route, is included in chapter 2. Maps and keys are included showing the public campgrounds near each of the major towns in the Panhandle. Maps and keys for the rest of the area covered in the book are in chapter 3.

The second part of the book gives advice on camping and backcountry travel in Alaska and the rest of the North. There are chapters on car camping, backpacking, canoe and kayak travel, ski touring, and mountaineering. Each of these includes a discussion on planning trips to Alaska in addition to a number of specific itineraries. One chapter is devoted to information on where to write if you have questions, want to buy tickets, make reservations, or need maps or other material.

Recommended Tours

Because there is so much to see in the North, it is difficult to decide how to spend limited amounts of time and money. Travel by automobile is lengthy, and those with limited vacation time may want to avoid the tedious drive to Alaska.

Travelers with only two or three weeks to spend should plan to travel at least one way by air. If possible, it is well worth while to go one way by ferry, making as many stopovers as time allows.

For families or individuals not wanting a strenuous backpacking trip, but desiring a real wilderness experience and a sampling of some of the finest scenery in the North, a two-week or month trip can be made in the Panhandle section of Alaska, perhaps including parts of the Yukon and British Columbia. Take the ferries from Seattle or Vancouver Island. You can save money and get reservations more easily if you leave your car. Make as many stops and side trips as you can, being sure to include Glacier Bay National Monument. Spend a week or two at one of the remote Forest

Service cabins. There are some near each of the Panhandle towns, approachable only by chartered boat or plane. Rent is $5 per night for the whole family. Reservations for the cabins have to be made well in advance, and information can be obtained from the Forest Service offices listed in chapter 11. At the northern end of the ferry system, Haines or Skagway, you can turn around, take a train to Whitehorse, or take a bus to the Yukon or the main part of Alaska.

Trips for backpackers and canoeists are recommended in the chapters on those subjects, but there are an infinite number of other possibilities. Trains in the North will let you off wherever you like and will pick you up weeks later; or you can charter an airplane and fly in to a remote lake region.

Those driving to Alaska should be sure to spend some time on the Kenai Peninsula and in McKinley National Park. These attractions should head the list of those to which one can drive. In the Yukon, be sure to plan to camp by Kluane Lake, one of the most beautiful of the northern lakes. Those drivers who feel comfortable on more remote roads may prefer to take the new Coast Range Highway, described in the next chapter. It by-passes the first part of the Alaska Highway and follows a more scenic route.

Alaska and her Canadian neighbors present enough variety for all those who love great and unspoiled places, whether they prefer relaxed family camping or rugged wilderness treks. Enjoy your trip to the North, help preserve the land for others, and good camping!

Acknowledgments

The maps in this book have been prepared using sheets of the United States Geological Survey, the Department of the Interior, and the Canadian Department of Mines and Technical Surveys, together with the author's own information.

I would like to thank all those friendly people I have met during my travels to Alaska, the Yukon, and British Columbia, particularly our Canadian neighbors, who seem unfailingly gracious and helpful.

1

Driving to Alaska

The most common way of getting to Alaska, the Yukon, or northern British Columbia is to drive, and this is the method of transportation most people planning a trip north are likely to consider. Before you commit yourself, however, it is well worth thinking about the other options available. The drive to Alaska is very long and time-consuming; the trip from San Francisco to Fairbanks, for example, is more than 3,200 miles, one way, with over 1,100 miles of gravel road. The Alaska Highway route is a worthwhile trip in many ways, but the scenery is not particularly interesting for much of that distance. If the more westerly route described here is taken, rain and poor road conditions must be considered as the norm. A trip using public transportation, perhaps with car rentals for some trips in the North, is often cheaper, and is certainly more economical of time if you have only a few weeks available for your vacation.

On the other hand, there is often an advantage to having one's own car available for side trips. Families or groups traveling together in a reliable and economical vehicle can make the trip more cheaply than in any other way, providing they camp most of the time. Finally, for the perceptive traveler, even tedious driving in some of the vast northern parts of the continent eventually conveys a true feeling for the size of the land.

The Alcan

Before World War II, there was no way to drive to Alaska. One could go by boat or air, or the hardy and adventurous could follow one of the overland routes blazed by trappers and gold-crazed prospectors. During the war, concern for the vulnerability of the northwestern part of the continent sparked a crash joint effort by the United States and Canada to build a road from Dawson Creek, British Columbia, through the Yukon Territory, to the state of Alaska. The resulting road, the Alcan, or Alaska Highway, has been periodically improved since, and it connects a number of population centers in Canada with roads in Alaska linking Anchorage, Fairbanks, and a number of other Alaskan communities. Side roads connect with various other outposts in the wilderness, including Dawson City in the Yukon and Canol in the Northwest Territories.

Pavement now extends almost one hundred miles from Dawson Creek and resumes again in Alaska. The connecting section, well over a thousand miles long, is a well graded and engineered gravel-surfaced road. It has been steadily improved over the years, a fact quite noticeable to those who have driven it several times, but it remains essentially a

(Top) The gravel road shown here is typical of the drive to Alaska. The roads are well graded and have a good surface, but it can deteriorate with rain or heavy truck traffic. There are many beautiful mountains and lakes along the way.

(Center) There are other features of interest besides natural ones on the drive to Alaska. This old sternwheel steamer used to carry freight and passengers on the Yukon River; now she has been restored and sits on dry ground at Whitehorse, capital of the Yukon Territory.

(Bottom) Water vapor rises from the hot springs runoff flats near the Liard River in northern British Columbia. The plant and fish life in the pools is unique.

wilderness highway. The surface will vary in quality from one place to another, depending on recent weather, truck traffic, and grading schedules. Though conditions have improved, the Alcan traveler must be prepared for dust, stones thrown up by passing trucks, and occasional chuckhole and washboard sections. After long periods of rain, conditions are likely to be worse, a possibility that has to be taken into account.

For those who are properly prepared, driving the Alcan can be a fascinating experience, and the highway provides access to some fine wilderness. There are many pitfalls, however, and drivers born and bred along modern superhighways will need to modify their expectations before driving north.

The route of the Alcan was deliberately chosen to follow the line of the least resistance. It stays well to the east and north of the main chain of the Rocky Mountain cordillera, so that for most of its length it avoids encounters with major mountains. Since the forests along the route are often dense, the scenery along much of the route is unspectacular. The forests themselves are often very attractive, particularly the beautiful stands of birch, but if the tourist expects the sort of views he has experienced in the Canadian Rockies, he is likely to be disappointed. The scenery becomes more interesting farther north, where for hundreds of miles the highway generally parallels the border between the Yukon and British Columbia, crossing back and forth between the two a number of times before finally edging decisively into the Yukon. There are a number of beautiful lakes and rivers along this section of the road. At Watson Lake, the Alcan is joined by the second land route, discussed below, and then the two cross the Cassiar Mountains, which divide the watersheds of the Mackenzie River, which drains into the Arctic Ocean, and the Yukon River, which travels all the way through Alaska to the Bering Sea.

Travelers camping on the Alaska Highway should not miss Liard River Hot Springs Provincial Park. The campground is lovely, and regardless of the hour you can soak away the aches of the road in the hot, spring-fed pools one quarter of a mile along the boardwalk from the campground. In the evening you can listen to local residents tell of the joys of leaping into the hot water when the air temperature is −50° F.

Once in the Yukon drainage, the highway passes several huge lakes: Teslin and Taku Arm, for example, which connect with others just as large. This whole area, which centers around Whitehorse, capital of the Yukon Territory, forms the headwaters of the Yukon River, and it is a paradise for canoeists and other water travelers. The road to Canol in the Northwest Territories leaves the Alcan at Teslin Lake, and the road to Dawson City leaves the highway at Whitehorse and loops north, finally rejoining the Alcan in Alaska.

Beyond Whitehorse, the highway begins to approach the Saint Elias Range, and it is here that one encounters the most spectacular scenery of the Alcan. Some of the smaller peaks

The Indians who live in the Yukon near the route of the Alcan build these miniature houses and shelters to house the spirits of their dead, who are buried here (milepost 974).

of the range rise above the town of Haines Junction, where the connecting road from the Alaska ferry system joins the Alaska Highway. The peaks above the road from here to the far end of the Kluane Lake are actually only the foothills of the mighty mountains beyond, which can be seen from some points of the highway. The greatest is the tremendous mass of Mount Logan (19,850 ft.), Canada's highest peak and North America's second highest. The area around Kluane Lake has long been a game refuge, and Dall sheep can often be seen from the highway near Kluane Lake. Much of the area is included in the new Kluane National Park, a fortunate state for one of the most beautiful lakes and wilderness areas of North America.

From Kluane Lake it is only a little over one hundred miles to the Alaska border and United States customs. (Canadian customs are at Beaver Creek, about twenty miles from the border.) In another eighty miles the traveler reaches Tetlin Junction, where the road that goes through Dawson City rejoins the Alcan, and in another thirteen miles, one comes to Tok, where the routes to Anchorage and Fairbanks split.

The Coast Range Road

Until the summer of 1973, the Alcan was the only way to drive to the Yukon, to Alaska, or to the northern part of British Columbia. Now, however, there is another route, since connecting roads have been built between the old Cassiar road, Telegraph Creek, Stewart, and the logging roads that join the Nass River Valley with the towns of Terrace and Kitwanga, in British Columbia near Prince Rupert.

This new road system is considerably more rugged than the present Alcan. There are only a few places to buy gas over the entire five hundred-mile length, and virtually the only place where one could get repairs would be at Stewart. Most of this road is fairly good, by back-road standards, but it should be driven at reasonable speeds, in a reliable vehicle, and with the realization that a breakdown will leave you a long way from mechanical help.

The road is far more interesting than the Alcan from a scenic point of view. The southern half is quite close to sections of the Coast Range, with countless spectacular

The camper will find far more solitude along the rougher Coast Range Road.

(Opposite, top) The intersections along the Coast Range Road are still not very well marked. This junction is known as the Nass Y. It is sixty miles from Terrace by the road from Columbia Cellulose plant and sixty-five miles by the Kalum Lake road (see the Coast Range Highway map). The left fork is a fascinating side trip to the mouth of the Nass River. To head north for Stewart or Alaska, bear right twice.

(Opposite, bottom) The junction with the Stewart Road, after which the road north is in better condition. Stewart is a worthwhile side trip, which may become necessary if you are low on gas. If you skip Stewart the next gasoline is 150 miles north—Tatogga Lake Resort, easy to miss.

(Above) Bridges along the southern part of the Coast Range Road are still fairly primitive. This one uses log stringers for support.

(Above) Once this publicly maintained part of the road is reached, one-lane steel bridges like this one are common.

(Below) This new bridge over the Stikine River had just opened when this picture was taken. It will be a two-lane bridge when completed, replacing the old ferry that can be seen at the left.

(Opposite) The area around the Todagin Mountain refuge makes fine country for backpacking, camping, and wildlife observation. By this point, the Coast Range Road has moved far enough inland to be in drier country, where heavy undergrowth and deadfall are less of a problem for the walker.

mountains visible from the road. The side road to Stewart takes the visitor down to the end of a long fjord that comes up to Stewart, a town served by the British Columbia Ferry System. The road continues by many lakes, past Mount Edziza Provincial Park, the Stikine River, and the access road to Telegraph Creek. The southern part of the road travels through dense rain forest, but farther north it works into the drier interior region. After passing through the Cassiar Mountains, the road finally meets the Alcan near Watson Lake, and the traveler to Alaska can still see the best scenery along the Alaska Highway as it lies beyond this intersection.

For those who want to drive to Alaska and feel sufficiently adventurous, the Coast Range Road (officially Provincial Road 37, except for the privately owned timber company section) is a far more interesting route than the Alcan. The scenery is spectacular, fishing is incredible, and crowds are still very much absent. Rain should be expected, however, and the traveler must be prepared to take care of himself and his vehicle. Towing charges from some parts of the route would undoubtedly exceed the value of many cars.

Preparing Your Vehicle for Driving North

The most important preparation you can make for a trouble-free trip is to make sure your vehicle is in good repair before you start. Everything should be tight at the beginning of your trip. Gravel roads have a way of shaking things loose anyway, so check all muffler brackets, front end attachments, and so forth, to make sure that they are in good repair and that all nuts and bolts are pulled tight. Shaky items that might last for tens of thousands of miles on pavement will be rapidly jolted loose on gravel.

Gas tanks are rather vulnerable to damage by rocks, and it is prudent to install a rubber mat to protect the underside of the tank. A piece of rubber floor mat, door mat, or truck mud flap will work nicely. You can either install it yourself or have a garage do it. Many establishments near the start of the Alcan specialize in protecting vehicles against gravel damage, though the work may be more expensive there than at home.

Make sure that shock absorbers are in good condition and that springs are not too soft or overloaded. These parts not only take a lot of beating themselves, but they protect other parts of your car from excessive wear. Heavy-duty shock absorbers will do a better job of handling chuckholes. Marginal tires are likely to blow out on gravel roads, and replacement will be expensive at roadside service stations. It is wise to have good tires on the car and to carry two good spares. If wheel rims become dented and will not hold air well, an inner tube can be installed in the tire to stop the leak.

Whether you choose to carry tools and spare parts will depend on your own feelings, on your skill at minor automotive repairs, and on the route you are taking. On the Alcan, you can depend on service stations to handle most problems, though they naturally have to charge more for parts than you would pay at home; they have high expenses and a short season. For this reason, many experienced travelers prefer to carry some tools and basic items themselves: electrical wiring items, plugs, points, ignition coil, distributor cap and rotor, fan belt, brake fluid, miscellaneous hardware, and spares or repair kits for generator, water pump, and fuel pump. Frequent changes of air filters, oil, and oil filters should be anticipated. Many of these items should be considered mandatory if you are planning to drive the Coast Range Road. Even if you are not very capable mechanically, you may be able to find a sympathetic soul who will help you put on a fan belt, but you are not likely to come across anyone who happens to have one of the right size in his hip pocket.

The items mentioned above fall in the category of minor repairs, and with a few exceptions, service stations within a reasonable distance on the major roads will be able to handle such parts and repairs if you cannot, without delaying your trip too much. At worst, unless you have an unusual vehicle, they will probably be able to get parts for common repairs from a few hundred miles away, though the cost will be higher than it would be at home.

It is important to remember that major repairs can be very expensive and very time-consuming. Though many mechanics in remote regions of Canada and Alaska have lots of ingenuity and skill in making repairs without standard parts, the manufacturers of automobiles are even more ingenious in the art of making such repairs impossible. Getting specialized parts shipped to a remote garage may consume most of your vacation and a large portion of your funds, so try to anticipate any problems your car might have. You'll have a more pleasant trip if you do.

At a less serious level, flying gravel and rocks can damage paint jobs, lights, and windows on your car. Many types of screen gravel shields, commercial and homemade, are used to protect the paint and chrome parts on the fronts of vehicles. The larger screens also give some protection to the windshields, though there is no effective way to protect the glass without dangerously limiting visibility. Screens and other protectors should not interfere with the beams of your headlights, which must be kept on at all times while you are driving on gravel.

The electrical system and battery of your car should be in good repair, both because reliability is important in sparsely settled regions, and because you are legally required to have your headlights on at all times when driving on gravel roads. This means your battery will not be charged as well as it is when you are driving on pavement. You should also devise some way to remind yourself to turn off the headlights when you leave the vehicle. Most people, not being accustomed to driving with headlights on in daylight, have a hard time remembering to turn them off. Don't trust your memory. A dead battery in a remote campground is a real inconvenience and with long northern days making it harder to notice your mistake, it is surprisingly easy to forget the lights. I use a length of string running from the light switch to the door handle as a reminder.

Windshield washers are a great convenience and safety feature on unpaved roads, whether wet or dry. If your car does not have them (or they don't work), consider installing a set.

Make sure that the jack(s) you have in your car work well and are versatile. Jacks that can only be made short enough to barely fit under the car with a flat may not fit under at all when the surface is irregular. Those that have a short range may be worthless when a ditch or soft shoulder requires that the car be jacked fairly high. A jack made to fit special jacking brackets on the car body becomes useless if the fixtures are bent, if the metal around them is rusted, or if the ground below that one point is soft. With any type of jack, a short piece of sturdy lumber should be carried to put under the bottom of the jack when the ground is soft.

Those who are traveling early or late in the season or who expect to use less frequented roads may want to consider carrying a shovel, chains, and a come-along winch.

Driving on Gravel Roads

If you would like to have a fairly trouble-free drive to Alaska, sensible driving is even more important than preparing your vehicle. Most people who come to grief from major mechanical problems have simply been driving too fast. The surfacing of the Alcan has become so much better in the last few years that it is often easy to drive at sixty miles per hour. This is illegal (speed limit on gravel highways in both Canada and Alaska is fifty) and it is imprudent for several reasons. Your car will suffer a lot more when you hit the inevitable chuckhole or washboard section. High speeds on gravel are very hard on tires. From the point of view of safety, gravel is a lot slipperier than dry pavement, and an emergency maneuver at high speed is likely to throw you out of control. Speeds of around forty-five or so on gravel are much easier on your car. Regardless of the speed you drive when the road is clear, please remember that your vehicle throws up a lot of gravel at high speeds, so when you are passing another car, slow down. You will also find that though trucks occasionally throw a rock at considerable velocity, most gravel is pitched up, but is not traveling horizontally; it is the speed of your own car that is most likely to break your windshield. If you slow down, you are far less likely to have to replace it.

Gravel roads don't have center stripes, but head-on collisions are just as damaging as they are on pavement, so, please, get in the habit of staying on your own side of the road. Last-minute swerves back onto the correct side are more likely to send your car into a skid on gravel.

Take extra care in wet weather. Traction will be poorer, and so will visibility; spray from a passing car or truck can suddenly blind you. Some parts of the road will be more affected than others, and the slippery area may occur just when you need to stop. You will find that water pools in chuckholes make it impossible to tell how deep the holes are, so slower driving will make the teeth-knocking jolt a little less jarring when you finally hit a deep hole that looked like a shallow puddle. Finally, there is one part of the Alcan (in the eastern Yukon) which passes over soil very heavy in clay. After prolonged rain, this stretch of road can be incredibly slick. Be careful.

Dust is always a problem on heavily used, unpaved roads. The present surfacing of the Alcan makes this less of a problem than it used to be, except in construction areas. Even so, if you are not accustomed to driving unpaved roads, you will find that there is still a lot of dust. Pack things that you want to stay clean, such as good clothes, in well-sealed containers. Plastic bags closed tightly with rubber bands do well. Keep the car windows closed, particularly when other vehicles are passing you or you are overtaking another car. If your blower has some kind of filter on the intake, leaving it on will pressurize the inside of the car somewhat and will greatly reduce the amount of dust that gets in. Avoid following other cars too closely, both to keep the air you are breathing cleaner and to improve visibility. Just slow down a little when you are overtaken by another vehicle, and both the problem of dust and the danger to your car from flying gravel will be reduced.

If your car breaks down for any reason, it will usually not be difficult to flag someone down for help, unless you are on a remote road. Custom in the North dictates that you stop for anyone having trouble, and this tradition is one worth upholding. If there is more than one person in a disabled car, it is prudent for someone to stay with it. Some highways in the North, particularly in Alaska, have more than their share of two-legged scavengers. Trailers are particularly vulnerable. If you have to leave the vehicle, lock it, get it as far off the road as possible, and leave a note for the authorities.

Other Items to Consider

Clearing Canadian customs is generally a routine matter. You should, of course, carry your registration papers for your vehicle, and a driver's license or some other identification for each member of the party. No passports are required. Naturalized citizens or alien residents of the United States should have copies of the appropriate papers. If the vehicle you are driving belongs to someone else, you should have some authorization from the owner to drive in Canada.

Canadian customs and immigration officials will want to know whether you have sufficient funds with you to complete your trip, with allowance for possible car trouble. They will probably ask how much money (including traveler's checks, cashier's checks, etc.) you have with you, and if they feel you are not prepared, they may deny entry.

Though British Columbia and the Yukon do not require it, it is prudent to get a card from your insurance company showing liability coverage in Canada. These are standard and usually are available without charge. Some eastern Canadian provinces require them for entry. You should also consider getting insurance coverage for possible theft of items from your car, usually as part of a homeowner's or renter's policy. Make a list of the items carried so that you can file a claim in case of theft, including serial numbers of such things as typewriters, cameras, and firearms. This list is also useful at customs.

Canadian customs regulations permit visitors to enter duty free with personal clothing and effects, recreational and camping equipment, two days' supply of food, two hundred cigarettes, two pounds of tobacco, fifty cigars, forty ounces of liquor or wine or two dozen twelve-ounce bottles of beer. Quantities in excess of these limits are dutiable, though in the case of food for wilderness trips, customs authorities are generally quite reasonable. Larger quantities can be taken through Canada by Americans en route to Alaska, providing they are carried in containers that can be easily sealed by customs to insure that the goods travel through Canada intact. The containers must then be checked out as you leave Canada. This same provision applies to handguns and fully automatic weapons, which are normally prohibited in Canada. Rifles and shotguns are allowed, but they must be registered at the border crossing, and, of course, appropriate laws regulating their use and transport must be observed.

On rare occasions, Canadian customs officers require a deposit on a dutiable item until it is taken out of the country, to be certain that it is not sold in Canada. However, this practice seems not to be used much with visitors traveling to and from Alaska.

Both Canadian and United States customs authorities are extremely touchy about the possibility of the importation of illegal drugs. For this reason, if you are carrying any medicines, see that they are properly labeled, and be sure to carry prescriptions, letters from doctors, or whatever else might be necessary to convince the most skeptical person of the identity of the drug and of the medical need for your carrying it in the quantity you have. Any unsuccessful attempt to circumvent Canadian customs regulations, particularly in the area of drugs, will result in an unceremonious ejection from the country.

Gasoline prices are high in the North, but they are also quite variable. They will generally be highest in the most remote locations. In spots that are not much frequented, one should also expect possible station closings late or early in the season. Supplies of premium fuel will not always be available, but this is not of too much consequence, since occasional running on lower octane gasoline will not cause any significant damage to the engine. New cars requiring unleaded fuel may present a more serious problem and it remains to be seen how well such fuel will be supplied in the North. If you are planning to drive a car with a catalytic converter (requiring unleaded gasoline) to Alaska, check in advance with auto club or tourist information sources to get detailed information on sources of unleaded fuel. Many travelers in the North like to carry some fuel in cans, both as a precaution and to enable them to buy most of their gasoline at the cheapest places. You should balance these advantages against the dangers posed by gasoline in an accident. At a minimum, the containers should be designed for flammable liquids. Don't use glass bottles or lightweight plastic jugs to carry gasoline. To reduce fuel costs, be sure to fill up whenever you find a place with reasonable prices, particularly when there will be no more communities of any size for some distance.

Though most businesses in Canada will accept American dollars, it is most economical to change currency at a bank. Also, remember in judging gas prices that Canada's imperial gallon is one-fifth larger than a United States gallon.

Specific Route Information

All the public campgrounds which existed at the time this book went to print have been listed. Those along the highways do not change much from one year to the next. Many establishments along the road also offer hookups for recreational vehicles, and no attempt has been made to list these. One can always camp anywhere that parking space for a car can be found, of course, but the campgrounds are generally far more pleasant. Some attempt has been made to indicate both the development and the pleasantness of the campgrounds, so that travelers will have some idea what to expect. None of these facilities is elaborate, and this fact should be borne in mind when one is forming expectations. A highly developed campsite along the Alaska Highway is one with drinking water, good gravel roads, marked and leveled sites, and picnic tables. Don't expect any hot showers.

Most northern highways, including the Alcan, are marked with mileposts giving a fairly reliable method for locating particular spots, though some posts may be missing, or the posts may be moved if construction reroutes a section of highway. Where mileposts do not exist, mileages are given from odometer readings, and these should be expected to differ considerably from one car to another.

The Alaska Highway and the Coast Range Road: Maps and Keys

The Alcan begins at Dawson Creek, British Columbia, milepost 0, but can also be reached by several side roads which come in within the first hundred miles, the most important coming from Hudson Hope, near the site of the W.A.C. Bennett Dam. The first map and key include campsites on these approaches.

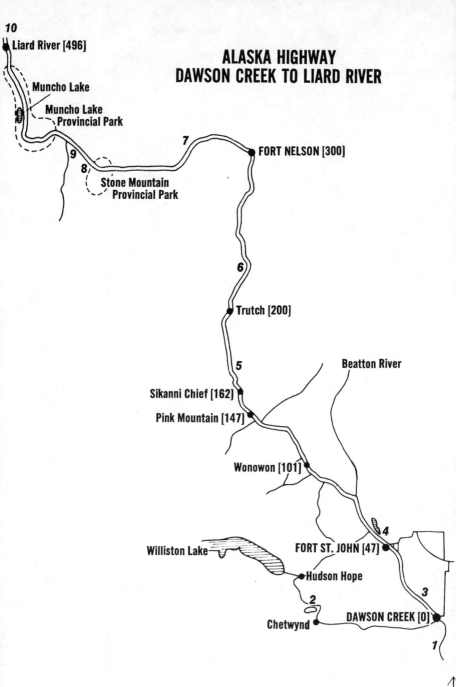

ALASKA HIGHWAY
DAWSON CREEK TO LIARD RIVER

10
Liard River [496]

Muncho Lake

Muncho Lake
Provincial Park

9

8

7

FORT NELSON [300]

Stone Mountain
Provincial Park

6

Trutch [200]

5

Beatton River

Sikanni Chief [162]

Pink Mountain [147]

Wonowon [101]

4

Williston Lake

FORT ST. JOHN [47]

Hudson Hope

3

2

Chetwynd

DAWSON CREEK [0]

1

N

Key to Campgrounds

1 **SUDETEN PARK** is a small campground and picnic area about 15 miles southeast of Dawson Creek on Highway 2. 15 spaces, drinking water.

2 **MOBERLY LAKE PARK** is a large and attractive campground on the lake. The access road is 2 to 3 miles long and leaves Highway 29 about 10 miles northwest of Chetwynd, 30 miles southeast of Hudson Hope. It is thus about 75 miles from Dawson Creek and 80 miles from the junction of Highway 29 with the Alaska Highway at milepost 54. 59 spaces, drinking water, dumping station. Swimming, fishing, boating in Moberly Lake. Boat launching ramp.

3 **KISKATINAW PARK** [20] is on the south bank of the Kiskatinaw River. 28 spaces, drinking water.

4 **CHARLIE LAKE PARK** [52] is situated a short distance from the lake. 58 campsites, drinking water, dumping station, boat launching ramp.

5 **BUCKINGHORSE RIVER PARK** [175] is near the river. 29 campsites, drinking water.

6 **PROPHET RIVER PARK** [222] is a modest stopover spot. 50 campsites, drinking water.

7 **KLEDO CREEK PARK** [335] is a very pleasant campground beside what is really a river. 51 campsites, drinking water.

8 **115 CREEK REST AREA** [403] is a small campground near Stone Mountain Park. 8 campsites, drinking water.

9 **RACING RIVER PARK** [418] is a pleasant campground located next to the river in good hiking country. 30 campsites, drinking water.

10 **LIARD RIVER HOT SPRINGS PARK** [496] is one of the most pleasant campsites anywhere. The boardwalk leading to the developed bathing pool, which is hot enough for year-round use, goes about ½ mile over some fascinating warm-water flats produced by runoff from the springs. There is a second pool about ¼ mile above the first, for those wishing more privacy—it is even hotter than the lower one. There are also some small

cold-water pools just above for those who like to shock
their circulatory systems. 21 campsites, drinking water,
dumping station, bathhouses at the lower pool.

Commercially operated campsites are located in Dawson Creek; at mileposts 41, 47, 49, 93, 102, 136, 146, 162,
295; at Fort Nelson (milepost 300); and at mileposts
308, 351, 397, 422, 442, and 463.

Fishing Information

HALFWAY RIVER is reached from an access road that turns
left off the Alcan 2 miles past the end of the pavement,
at milepost 95. It has good fishing for rainbows and
Dolly Varden.

BUCKINGHORSE RIVER, on which campground 5 is
located at milepost 175, has grayling and northern pike.

BEAVER RIVER, crossed by the Alcan at milepost 206, has
good fishing for rainbows and grayling.

PROPHET RIVER, which parallels the highway from the
campground at milepost 222 all the way to Fort Nelson
at milepost 300, has good trout fishing as do a number of
its tributaries over which the highway passes in this
section.

MACDONALD RIVER, at milepost 397, has grayling and
Dolly Varden.

RACING RIVER, next to the campground at milepost 418,
has good fishing for grayling and Dolly Varden.

TOAD RIVER, which parallels the highway from milepost
429 and crosses it at 437, has Dolly Varden.

MUNCHO LAKE, beside the Alcan from mileposts 456 to
465, is a good place to fish for lake trout. It also has
grayling and whitefish.

TROUT RIVER, crossed on a bridge at milepost 476, has
whitefish and grayling.

LIARD RIVER, crossed at milepost 496, has whitefish,
grayling, and Dolly Varden.

ALASKA HIGHWAY
LIARD RIVER TO WHITEHORSE

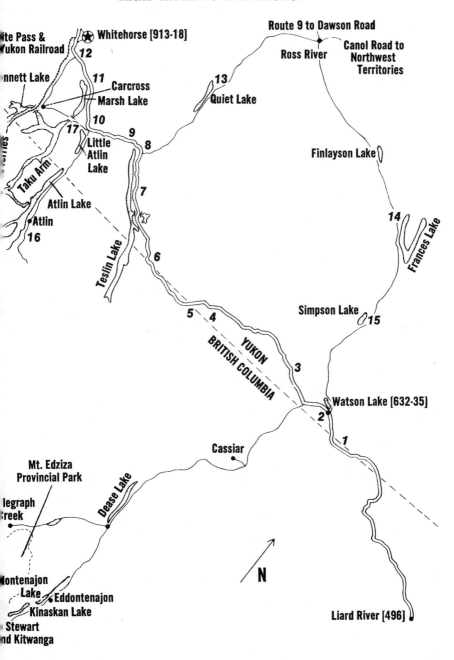

Route 9 to Dawson Road

Ross River

Canol Road to
Northwest
Territories

te Pass &
ukon Railroad

Whitehorse [913-18]

12

11

Carcross

Marsh Lake

13

Quiet Lake

nnett Lake

10

17

9

8

Little
Atlin
Lake

Finlayson Lake

Taku Arm

7

Atlin Lake

Frances Lake

14

Atlin

16

Teslin Lake

6

5 4

YUKON

BRITISH COLUMBIA

Simpson Lake

15

3

Watson Lake [632-35]

2

1

Cassiar

Mt. Edziza
Provincial Park

Dease Lake

legraph
reek

ontenajon
Lake

Eddontenajon

Kinaskan Lake

Stewart
nd Kitwanga

N

Liard River [496]

Key to Campgrounds

1   **HYLAND RIVER PARK** is at milepost 606 by the river. There are 37 campsites and drinking water.

2   **WATSON LAKE CAMPGROUND** is near milepost 632 on the south side of the road, a little before one enters the town of Watson Lake. It has drinking water, a dumping station, and 45 spaces.

3   **BIG CREEK CAMPGROUND** is at milepost 674 on the north side of the road, near the bridge going over the creek. There are 30 spaces.

4   **RANCHERIA CAMPGROUND** is just past the town of that name. The access road goes off to the south right after milepost 710. The campground is on the river and has a dumping station and 30 spaces.

5   **SEAGULL CREEK CAMPGROUND (SWIFT RIVER CAMPGROUND)** is on the south side of the highway past milepost 732 and has 10 spaces.

6   **MORLEY RIVER CAMPGROUND** is on the north side of the highway just before milepost 777 and after the turnoff for Morley Lake. There are 30 spaces.

7   **TESLIN LAKE CAMPGROUND** is at milepost 813 next to the lake on the south side of the highway, about ten miles past the town of Teslin. It has a dumping station, an attractive view, and 30 spaces.

8   **JOHNSON'S CROSSING CAMPGROUND** is beside the Teslin River just past milepost 837 and a mile past the junction with the Canol Road. A boat ramp and 30 spaces are available.

9   **SQUANGA LAKE CAMPGROUND** is past milepost 849 on the north side of the highway by the lake. It has a dumping station and 30 spaces.

10 **JUDAS CREEK CAMPGROUND** is at milepost 872 on the north side of the highway near the bridge over the creek. There are 30 spaces.

11 **MARSH LAKE CAMPGROUND** is at milepost 890 on the south side of the road at the west end of the lake,

which is more attractive than its name. It has drinking water, a dumping station, and 30 spaces.

12   **WOLF CREEK CAMPGROUND** is at milepost 906 by the bridge over the creek on the north side of the highway. There are a dumping station, drinking water, and 50 spaces.

Campground on the Canol Road (Yukon Highway 8)

13   **QUIET LAKE CAMPGROUND** is about 50 miles along the Canol Road, at the north end of the lake, to the west of the road. Note that no gas is available until Ross River, another 100 miles north. There are 10 spaces.

Campgrounds on the Watson–Carmacks Road
(Yukon Highway 9)

14   **FRANCES LAKE CAMPGROUND** is east of the road on the north end of this very large lake. It is about 105 miles north of Watson Lake and 125 miles from Ross River. There are 10 spaces. Note that there is no gas available for the 230 miles between Watson Lake and Ross River.

15   **SIMPSON LAKE CAMPGROUND** is on a short side road leading west from the highway about 50 miles from Watson Lake and 180 from Ross River. There are 20 spaces.

Campground on the Atlin Road
(Yukon Highway 7 to British Columbia)

16   **ATLIN CAMPGROUND** is located at the north end of the village of Atlin, a short distance from the lake. The road to Atlin turns off the Alcan at milepost 866, Jake's Corner. After a mile, the Atlin road bears left, while the right fork goes to Carcross and back to the Alaska Highway near Whitehorse. Atlin is about 60 miles south, back across the border in British Columbia.

Campground on the Carcross Loop (Yukon Highways 5 and 6)

17   **TAGISH BRIDGE CAMPGROUND** is located on the side loop which goes from Jake's Corner, milepost 866 on the Alaska Highway, west through Tagish a total of 35 miles to Carcross, and then north another 49 miles to meet the Alcan again between mileposts 904 and 905, near Whitehorse. The campground is located 13 miles from Jake's Corner. Turn south, and then turn right at the fork a mile along the road. (The left branch goes to Atlin.) The campground has 40 spaces, a boat ramp, and a dumping station.

Commercially operated campsites are operated at mileposts 533, 543, 596; in Watson Lake (632–35); at mileposts 642, 721, 797, 806, 813, 904, 911; and in Whitehorse (913–18).

Fishing Information

SOUTH TEETER CREEK, which is crossed beyond milepost 501, has grayling and Dolly Varden. A trail leads north, upstream, to a falls.

SMITH RIVER is crossed by a bridge at milepost 513. There is good fishing for grayling and Dolly Varden along the trail leading upstream to the north.

HYLAND RIVER, next to the campground of that name at milepost 606, is a good place to fish for grayling and Dolly Varden.

WATSON LAKE, north of the town at milepost 633, has trout and grayling.

UPPER LIARD RIVER is crossed by the road past milepost 642. When it is clear, there is good fishing for grayling, Dolly Varden, whitefish, and northern pike.

RANCHERIA RIVER first crosses the Alcan at milepost 687 and is accessible at a number of points to milepost 722, including the campground near 710. It has good fishing for grayling and Dolly Varden.

SWIFT RIVER, crossed at mileposts 725 and 733, has grayling.

MORLEY LAKE, reached by a turnoff around milepost 776, has good fishing for lake trout and northern pike.

MORLEY RIVER, by the campground near milepost 777, has good grayling and Dolly Varden fishing.

TESLIN LAKE, by which the road runs between mileposts 800 and 837, has excellent fishing for lake trout, grayling, northern pike, sheefish, salmon, and whitefish.

TESLIN RIVER, by the Johnson's Crossing Campground at milepost 837, has grayling and, around mid-August, king salmon.

SQUANGA LAKE, next to the campground at milepost 849, has good fishing for whitefish, grayling, and northern pike.

MARSH LAKE, by the campground at milepost 890, has lake trout, grayling, and northern pike.

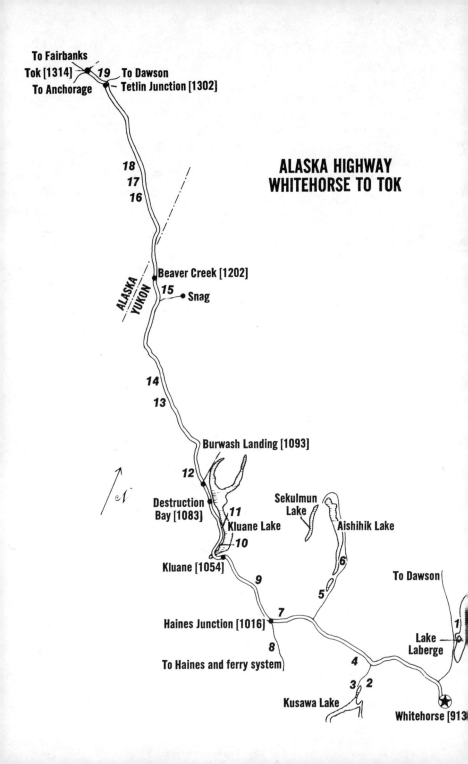

ALASKA HIGHWAY
WHITEHORSE TO TOK

To Fairbanks
Tok [1314]
To Anchorage
19
To Dawson
Tetlin Junction [1302]

18
17
16

ALASKA
YUKON

Beaver Creek [1202]
15
Snag

14
13

Burwash Landing [1093]

12

Destruction
Bay [1083]
11
Kluane Lake
10

Sekulmun
Lake
Aishihik Lake

Kluane [1054]
9
6
5
To Dawson

7
Haines Junction [1016]
1
Lake
Laberge

8
To Haines and ferry system
4

3 2
Kusawa Lake
Whitehorse [913]

Key to Campgrounds

1 **LAKE LABERGE** is off the highway going north to Dawson (Yukon Highway 2). Turn north from the Alcan just beyond milepost 925, and continue past new milepost 20. After ½ mile, a side road goes 2 miles east to the campground on Lake Laberge. 60 spaces, drinking water, dumping station. Swimming, boating, boat launching ramp at the lake.

2 **TAKHINI RIVER PICNIC GROUND** is 15 miles south of the Alcan. The turnoff is past milepost 958.

3 **KUSAWA LAKE CAMPGROUND** is another 2 miles beyond Takhini River Picnic Ground. There are 40 spaces, with swimming and boating in the lake.

4 **MENDENHALL CREEK CAMPGROUND** is on the south side of the road just past milepost 968 and a lodge and gas station. There are 30 campsites.

5 **OTTER FALLS CAMPGROUND** is 18 miles north up the side road that leaves the Alcan just beyond milepost 995. The falls themselves are very beautiful; they are the ones engraved on the back of Dominion five-dollar bills. 10 spaces.

6 **AISHIHIK LAKE CAMPGROUND** is another 10 miles beyond Otter Falls. The road is unreliable beyond Otter Falls and its condition should be checked carefully, particularly beyond Aishihik Lake Campground; it is another 46 miles beyond to the abandoned village at the end of the lake. Check in advance at the repeater station near the Aishihik River Bridge on the Alcan, a little over a mile beyond the turnoff (just beyond milepost 996). There is a boat ramp at the Aishihik Lake Campground, which has 6 spaces.

7 **PINE CREEK CAMPGROUND** is on the north side of the Alcan at milepost 1013, a little before Haines Junction. 30 spaces, with a dumping station.

8 **KATHLEEN LAKE CAMPGROUND** is 17 miles south of Haines Junction on the road to Haines. There are 30 spaces at this lovely spot, with a boat launching ramp.

9   **SULPHUR LAKE CAMPGROUND** is past milepost 1038. There are 10 sites.

10   **KLUANE LAKE CAMPGROUND** is one of the most beautiful in the North. It is on the shore of the lake, just beyond milepost 1064. There are about 40 spots and there is a dumping station.

11   **GOOSE BAY CAMPGROUND** is also on the shore of Kluane Lake, beyond milepost 1072. There are 10 sites.

12   **BURWASH FLATS CAMPGROUND** is near the north end of Kluane Lake, near milepost 1105. There are 30 places and drinking water.

13   **LAKE CREEK CAMPGROUND** is on the southwest side of the highway near milepost 1152. There are 30 places and drinking water.

14   **PICKHANDLE LAKE**, by milepost 1158, is primarily a picnic ground, though one can also camp there. There is a boat ramp.

15   **SNAG JUNCTION CAMPGROUND** is just before milepost 1189, about $\frac{1}{4}$ mile beyond the junction with the side road to Snag. There are 20 places and a dumping station.

16   **GARDINER CREEK WAYSIDE** is on the southwest side of the Alcan beyond milepost 1246. It is not a terribly attractive campground. There are 6 sites.

17   **DEADMAN CREEK WAYSIDE**, despite the name, is a fairly pleasant campground, except in wet weather, when the site does not drain well. The access road goes off near milepost 1249. It has a boat ramp and 16 campsites.

18   **LAKEVIEW WAYSIDE** is a pretty spot with a boat ramp, located just before milepost 1257. There are 6 campsites.

19   **TOK RIVER WAYSIDE** is located on the riverbank just past milepost 1309, about 5 miles before the town of Tok. There are 10 campsites.

Fishing Information

MENDENHALL CREEK, by the campground at milepost 968, has grayling.

OTTER FALLS area, by the campground on the side road leaving the Alcan at milepost 995, has excellent fishing for rainbow and grayling.

AISHIHIK LAKE, by the campground farther up the same side road, has good fishing for lake trout.

KLUANE LAKE, which the highway parallels from about mileposts 1054 to 1100, has fine fishing for whitefish, lake trout, and northern pike. Some of the tributaries provide good grayling and trout fishing when they are clear.

DEADMAN LAKE, beside the campground at milepost 1249, has rainbows and northern pike.

2

The Ferries and the Marine Highway

One of the most attractive ways to get to Alaska and the Yukon is via the system of ferries that follows the coast from Seattle, Washington, to the ports of Haines and Skagway in Alaska. These ferries generally follow what is known as the Inland Passage, a salt water route that is protected from ocean storms by the great chain of islands that stretches along the coastline of British Columbia and southeastern Alaska.

There are several advantages to the ferry route. The scenery is as fine as any in the world, ranging from lush northern rain forests to huge glaciers and gigantic peaks. The only way that one can reach any of the towns of the Alaska Panhandle (the southern coastal extension of the state) or many similar villages in British Columbia is by ferry or by plane. What roads exist simply run along the coast a little way and stop. One cannot drive to Juneau, the current capital of Alaska, for example. This lack of highway access is one of the great charms of these towns. They are quieter and less affected by the oil boom economy than cities like Anchorage and Fairbanks. Finally, the ferry route avoids the disadvantages of the long drive along the Alaska Highway, as far as Haines Junction. The highway is joined where its scenery is best, as it approaches the Saint Elias Range.

One common misconception should be laid to rest immediately. *The ferries do not go to the main part of Alaska.* From the northernmost port of call of the boats, one must still take a car, bus, or plane to get to Anchorage, Fairbanks, McKinley

45

The country around the Marine Route tends to be precipitous and heavily forested. There are many glaciers, and when strong rock bands form cliffs, there are waterfalls like these.

Park, or wherever. This is because the protective chain of islands ends near Haines and Skagway, and the violent weather of the Gulf of Alaska presents severe navigational problems. Anyone wishing to continue north can take a car or other vehicle along on the ferry, or arrange to use public transportation from Haines or Skagway. A train can be taken from Skagway to Whitehorse, capital of the Yukon.

There are two ferry systems operating in the area, one run by the Province of British Columbia and the other by the State of Alaska, and in addition, there are some privately operated steamer routes. There is some overlapping between the two ferry systems and probably the nicest trips combine their use. The Alaska state ferries operate from Seattle, Washington, Prince Rupert, British Columbia, and the major Alaskan towns in the Panhandle: Ketchikan, Wrangell, Petersburg, Sitka, Juneau, Haines, and Skagway. Not all the ferries stop at all points: those which stop at Sitka dock at Auke Bay rather than Juneau, the latter two being about fourteen miles apart and connected by road. A new vessel in the Alaska ferry system will also provide service to Hoonah and Kake.

The British Columbia ferries connect Vancouver, various ports on Vancouver Island, and coastal towns of British Columbia, such as Prince Rupert. Besides the fact that the British Columbia ferries stop at a number of interesting ports that are not served by the Alaska ferry system, they also offer the advantage of being considerably cheaper. Those trying to pinch pennies on an Alaska trip and planning on taking ferries in one direction or both may wish to take the British Columbia ships from the Seattle-Vancouver area to Prince Rupert and change to the Alaska system there.

Stopovers, Reservations, Automobiles, and Accommodations

All the ferries can carry vehicles, the charge generally being determined by the length of the automobile, camper, car and trailer, or truck. There are height restrictions on some ships and schedules include details. In general, one can carry as much luggage in the vehicle as one wishes, but passengers may not ride or sleep in their cars. Pets on the Alaska ferries must be transported in vehicles or in special traveling cases on the auto deck, and they must be cared for by their owners. Access to the car deck is limited; owners must be accompanied by crew members when going to their cars.

The main expense in traveling on the ferry system is auto transportation. Individual fares are quite reasonable. For example, in summer of 1975, the fare for an individual from Prince Rupert to Haines was $48 and the vehicle charge for a passenger car was $140. Hence, a trip without an automobile can be much more economical, providing public transportation can be arranged for other segments of one's trip.

Rates change on both ferry systems, as do schedules, so one should write for current information to the addresses given in chapter 11. In considering overall cost, the prospective tourist should take into account the mileage. Those approaching from east of the Rockies will have to drive much farther to get to Seattle, Vancouver, or Prince Rupert than they would to get to the start of the Alcan at Dawson Creek, and the extra mileage will raise the cost of the trip both in money and time. On the other hand, west coast residents will not need to travel nearly as far to reach the southern termini of the Marine Highway as they would to get to the Alaska Highway.

During the height of the season, places on the ferries are in considerable demand, particularly for those who are bringing cars or who want cabin space. Basic fare includes transporta-

The Marine Route also passes many picturesque towns, surrounded by heavily forested slopes.

tion only, and if the passenger wishes to sleep, he has to bundle up in a deck chair. If berths are desired, they run approximately an extra $25 each from Seattle to Haines, depending on the number of berths per cabin and the particular ship. Meals are also extra.

If you are traveling at the height of the season and wish to take your car or have cabin space, it is important to make advance reservations as soon as possible, since there are more places on all the ferries for passengers than there are berths or vehicle spaces. Space is tightest northbound in May and June, southbound in late August and early September. Unfortunately, you will have to plan your exact itinerary in advance to make reservations. You may or may not be able to get changes made later if you decide you would like to stay longer at one place and spend less time at another.

There are no additional charges made for stopovers at the various Alaskan ports, and this is one real boon for the traveler. On one trip along the Marine Highway, you can stop at as many of the towns along the way as you have time for. You must plan your stops in advance if you are taking a car, however, since it will be loaded for a particular port, and there will be no way to get it off if you suddenly decide you would like to stop over at another place after all.

There are possibilities for hiking, camping, and side trips at each of the stopovers on the Marine Highway. One can charter a plane or smaller boat and spend a week on a wilderness island, climb a nearby mountain, or lounge at a local campground. You should plan for rainy weather, however. Ketchikan often gets as much rain in a month as San Francisco does in a year.

Recommended Trips

Despite the risk of bad weather, anyone planning a trip north who has the time should ride the ferries at least one way, making as many stopovers as possible. Some of the most charming towns in the North are in this area, and the scenery is as spectacular as any in the world. The opportunity for side trips is virtually unlimited. There are many Forest Service cabins in this region which are accessible only by float plane and which can be rented for $5 per night for the entire party.

Northland Navigation Steamers from Prince Rupert go up the so-called Portland Canal, a long inlet, to Stewart. This is a fine side trip in good weather, and the canal forms the southern border between Alaska and Canada. Some of the mountains which rise from this fjord are nearly nine thousand feet high, a spectacular rise from the sea. Until quite recently,

Stewart could only be reached by plane or boat, but it is now possible to drive.

There are Forest Service and other campgrounds accessible by road from all the Alaskan towns served by the main ferry system: Ketchikan, Wrangell, Petersburg, Sitka, and Juneau. The campgrounds are shown on the accompanying maps, but for those traveling without cars, they are often hard to get to, unless one can get a ride or relishes long walks on the road. Adventurous travelers may want to take bicycles along on the ferry. The road systems around the Panhandle towns are fairly short, making them very suitable for touring by bicycles equipped for wet weather. At the end of the ferry trip, bikes can be shipped home, stored to await the return trip, or packed up and taken along.

Besides trips to Forest Service cabins, there are many other worthwhile side trips that can be arranged in planes or small boats. A boat trip up the Stikine River from the town of Wrangell is fascinating from both historical and scenic perspectives. The route was one of those followed inland by gold seekers. The Indians who preceded them and stayed after they were gone still live largely by fishing upriver at Telegraph Creek. The mountains rising above the Stikine form one of the finest glaciated valleys in the world.

From Juneau one can charter a boat or plane to Admiralty Island, a spectacular land of rain forests of spruce and hemlock, which has a very large population of grizzlies and more bald eagles than the rest of the United States put together. Small boats can negotiate lakes or inlets on the island. Hiking is feasible but very rugged because of rain and dense forest growth. There are a number of Forest Service cabins on the island.

Juneau is also the jump-off place for Glacier Bay National Monument, the largest and one of the most spectacular units

Steep mountains, glaciers, dense forests, and a lot of rain are characteristic of the Alaska Panhandle and the coast of British Columbia.

in the national park system. The boat tour of Glacier Bay is guided by ranger-naturalists and is very worthwhile. The tour boat can drop campers and backpackers off along one of the inlets with arrangements to pick them up later on. (If you make plans to do this, be sure to take extra food, since on days when large amounts of ice break off from the glacier at the head of the inlet, the waters may not be navigable until some of the ice cakes have been carried out by the tide. Hence, the boat may be a day or two late picking you up.) One can also camp near park headquarters. The monument can only be reached by boat or plane, and trailers or pickups cannot be transported, so campers have to have reasonably portable tents. Park headquarters and a lodge operated by a concessioner are located at Bartlett Cove. Besides charter boats and planes, there is regular air service to Glacier Bay from Juneau by Alaska Airlines, and planes arrive early enough in the morning to be in time for the daily boat tour. One can also explore the various inlets by small boat, of course, but owners should consult with park rangers first about safety precautions. Kayaks or canoes can be taken into one of the inlets on the tour boats and used for a few days' exploration. All small craft should stay well away from the heads of the glaciers, since the pieces of ice that break off are so huge that the waves they cause can easily swamp a boat—half a mile is a safe distance.

The scenery at Glacier Bay is awesome. Huge glaciers wind down to the sea, forming vast ice cliffs at the head of each inlet, with great towers periodically breaking off the snouts and falling into the ocean. The monument also provides striking examples of plant succession and of the speed with which the glaciers have been receding. The cabin built three-quarters of a century ago by John Muir, the great naturalist, was at the tongue of the glacier at the time, but it is now tens of miles back along the inlet. As the glaciers recede, they leave bare and sterile earth, composed mainly of gravel and rock. Soon plants begin to grow, and as one travels along the shores of the bay, the succession can be easily seen, from the first brave mosses and fireweeds establishing outposts of life in the middle of barren ground, through the outposts of dryas and alder, to the magnificent climax forests of hemlock and spruce. Glacier Bay is one trip that no one visiting the Panhandle area should miss.

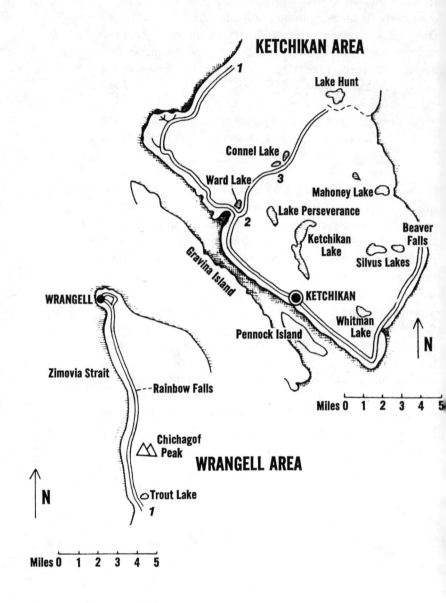

KETCHIKAN AREA

1

Lake Hunt

Connel Lake

Ward Lake

3

Mahoney Lake

Lake Perseverance

2

Ketchikan
Lake

Beaver
Falls

Gravina Island

Silvus Lakes

KETCHIKAN

Whitman
Lake

Pennock Island

N

Miles 0 1 2 3 4 5

WRANGELL

Zimovia Strait

Rainbow Falls

Chichagof
Peak

WRANGELL AREA

N

Trout Lake

1

Miles 0 1 2 3 4 5

Key to Campgrounds

1   **SETTLERS' COVE CAMPGROUND** is at the end of the road leading north from the town of Ketchikan, known as the North Tongass Highway. The campground is 18 miles from town. It has about 20 places and is situated in a beautiful spot near the beach. Drinking water and a boat ramp are available.

2   **SIGNAL CREEK CAMPGROUND and CCC CAMPGROUND** are located by Ward Lake, a mile up the Ward Lake Road from the North Tongass Highway. Signal Creek is the main campground, with 25 spaces, and is reached first. It has drinking water. CCC is a small campground $\frac{1}{4}$ mile farther down the road, with 4 spaces.

3   **LAST CHANCE CAMPGROUND** is 3 miles up the Ward Lake Road near Ward Creek. It has 23 spaces and drinking water.

Key to Campgrounds

1   **PAT'S CREEK CAMPGROUND** is located 11 miles from town at the end of the road that runs south from Wrangell. There are 9 sites.

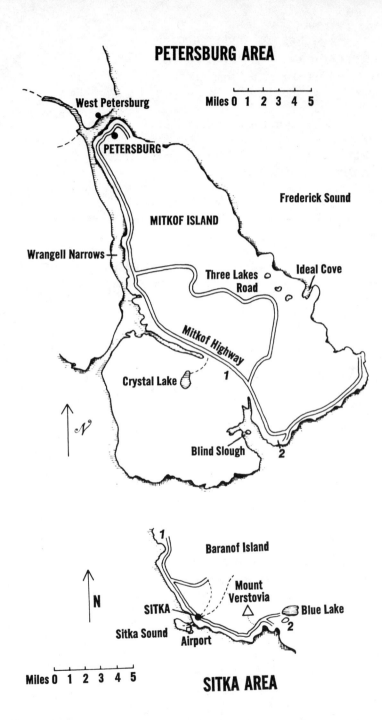

PETERSBURG AREA

Miles 0 1 2 3 4 5

West Petersburg

PETERSBURG

Frederick Sound

MITKOF ISLAND

Wrangell Narrows

Three Lakes Road

Ideal Cove

Mitkof Highway

1

Crystal Lake

N

Blind Slough

2

1

Baranof Island

N

Mount Verstovia

Blue Lake

SITKA

Sitka Sound

Airport

2

Miles 0 1 2 3 4 5

SITKA AREA

Key to Campgrounds

1 **OHMER CREEK CAMPGROUND** is 20 miles south of Petersburg on the Mitkof Highway. There are 15 sites and drinking water.

2 **SUMNER STRAITS CAMPGROUND** is near the beach 25 miles south of Petersburg on the Mitkof Highway. There are 20 places.

Key to Campgrounds

1 **STARRIGAVAN CAMPGROUND** is 8 miles north of town near the bay of the same name. It is less than a mile north of the ferry terminal. There are 29 campsites, most on the hill to the east of the road, with a few toward the beach.

2 **SAWMILL CREEK CAMPGROUND** is 6 miles from town, a mile down a side road going off the Blue Lake Road, which leads east from Sitka. There are 6 sites and drinking water.

Eagle Glacier

JUNEAU AREA

Windfall Lake

Montana Creek Trail

McGinnis Mountain △

Mendenhall Glacier

Peterson Lake

△ Bullard Mountain

1

Mendenhall Lake

2

Auke Lake

Airport

△ Juneau Mountain

N

△ Mount Troy

✶ JUNEAU

DOUGLAS ISLAND

3

Thane

△ Hawthorne Peak

Sunny Co

△ Mount Bradley

Miles 0 1 2 3 4 5

Key to Campgrounds

1   **MENDENHALL LAKE CAMPGROUND** is a large facility in a spectacular (and slightly chilly) setting below the Mendenhall Glacier and the peaks surrounding it. Take the road leading north from Juneau (or south from the other ferry terminal at Auke Bay). The Mendenhall Road forms a loop meeting the highway 9 miles northeast of town and again 12 miles from the center of Juneau. Taking either cutoff leads to a side road to the campground, 4 miles from the first cutoff after Juneau or 2 miles from the second cutoff. There are 65 sites and drinking water.

2   **AUKE VILLAGE CAMPGROUND** is 16 miles from Juneau along the road leading northeast along the coast, about two miles past the Auke Bay ferry terminal. The campground is near the beach and has 11 sites and drinking water.

3   **SANDY BEACH RECREATION AREA** is near the small boat harbor of Douglas, across the bridge from Juneau on the other side of the Gastineau Channel. It has a dumping station and drinking water, and camping is permitted; but the site is suitable mainly for vehicle campers using the parking lot.

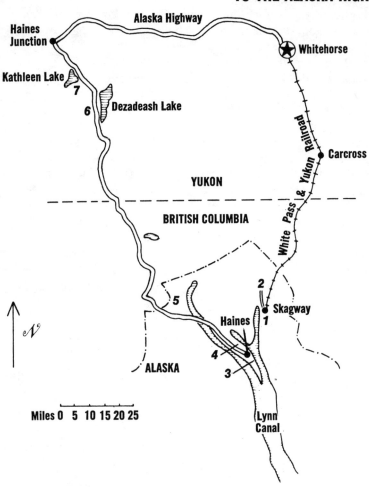

ROUTES FROM FERRY SYSTEM
TO THE ALASKA HIGHWAY

Alaska Highway

Haines
Junction

Whitehorse

Kathleen Lake

7

6   Dezadeash Lake

White Pass & Yukon Railroad

Carcross

YUKON

BRITISH COLUMBIA

N

5

2

Skagway

Haines

1

4

3

ALASKA

Miles 0   5 10 15 20 25

Lynn
Canal

Key to Campgrounds

1 **SKAGWAY CITY PARK** is at the end of Broadway. There are 10 sites and drinking water.

2 **LIARSVILLE WAYSIDE** is located about 3 miles north of the center of town and about 1½ miles north of the ferry terminal. There are 7 spots.

3 **PORTAGE COVE CAMPGROUND** is 2 miles southeast of Haines on the Beach Road. There are 9 sites.

4 **CHILKOOT LAKE CAMPGROUND** is on the road that runs north from Haines to the ferry terminal, 10 miles from Haines and 5 miles beyond the terminal. It is a beautiful campground with 32 sites, a boat ramp, and drinking water.

5 **MOSQUITO LAKE WAYSIDE** is on a side road two miles east off the main road to the Alcan, 27 miles from Haines (132 miles from Haines Junction). It has 10 sites.

6 **DEZADEASH LAKE CAMPGROUND** is 127 miles from Haines (32 from Haines Junction) halfway along the shore of the lake. There are 12 sites.

7 **KATHLEEN LAKE CAMPGROUND** is on a beautiful lake on a side road to the west 142 miles from Haines and 17 miles from Haines Junction. It has a dumping station, a boat ramp, and 20 spaces.

3

Camping Guide to Other Areas in the North

In the first two chapters, maps with keys to campgrounds have been included for the Alaska Highway, the Coast Range Highway, and the Panhandle of Alaska, which is served by the ferry systems. This chapter consists of a map and a key to other areas of the North which are accessible by road, together with some information on more remote areas.

All along the roads of the North there are good places to pitch your tent for the night, get out the backpacks, and take off for a few days or a few weeks.

ALASKA

- 65 • Circle
- 63
- 64
- 60 • Livengood
- 62
- Manley Hot Springs 61
- **FAIRBANKS**
- 5
- • Chena Hot Springs
- Nenana
- 4
- 3 • Delta Junction
- 2
- McKinley Park
- 66
- 57 55 54
- 58 56
- 59
- 67
- 1 • Tok
- Mount McKinley National Park
- Mt. McKinley △△
- 78
- 6
- 77
- 68 Paxson
- 7
- Petersville • Talkeetna
- 69
- 10
- 8
- N ↑
- 11
- 9 Glennallen
- Wasilla
- 14
- 53 18
- 16
- 17
- 15 13 12
- 52 51
- Palmer
- 71
- 72
- 70
- **ANCHORAGE**
- 19
- 20
- 21
- 22
- 23
- Portage
- Valdez
- 74 73
- 75
- 28
- 24
- 25
- Kenai 42
- 41
- Hope 26
- 27
- 29
- Cordova
- Soldotna
- 40 37
- 30
- 76
- 44 43
- 39 38
- 32
- 45 46
- 36 35 31
- 33
- 47
- **KENAI**
- 34 Seward
- 48
- **PENINSULA**
- Montague Island
- 49 50
- Homer
- Kayak Island
- Seldovia •
- **GULF OF ALASKA**

Key to Campgrounds

Campgrounds Along the Continuation
of the Alaska Highway—Tok to Fairbanks

1 **MOON LAKE WAYSIDE** is off the road by the lake near milepost 1332; it is near the Tanana River. There are 13 sites and a boat launching ramp.

2 **CLEARWATER-ALCAN WAYSIDE** is 8 miles up a side road which goes off to the right just before milepost 1415. It is a very pleasant spot on the Clearwater River, with 12 sites and a boat ramp.

3 **BIG DELTA CAMPGROUND** is just off the road to the right near milepost 1423 in a wooded area. It has drinking water and 24 campsites.

4 **HARDING LAKE RECREATION AREA** is located a little past milepost 1477, about 40 miles from Fairbanks. There are a boat ramp, a dumping station, drinking water, and 89 campsites.

5 **GROWDEN PARK** and **CHENA RIVER WAYSIDE** provide camping within the city of Fairbanks, both with water and restrooms. The former is located at Second Avenue and Wilbur with about 50 places, and the latter is on University Avenue by the river, just off Airport Way, with 67 campsites.

Commercially operated campgrounds along this section of the highway are situated in Tok; near mileposts 1327, 1412, and 1490; and in Fairbanks.

Campgrounds Between Tok and Anchorage
(Glenn Highway)

6 **EAGLE TRAIL WAYSIDE** is about 16 miles past Tok. There are 40 campsites and drinking water.

7 **PORCUPINE CREEK WAYSIDE** is a short distance off the road on the north side, near a bridge crossing the creek about 61 miles from Tok. It has 12 sites and drinking water.

8   **DRY CREEK WAYSIDE** is 136 miles from Tok, 11 miles past Gakona Junction, where the Richardson Highway comes in from the north, and about 5 miles north of Glennallen. It is at the site of an old Indian village, and there are burial plots in the area. (Please do not disturb them.) There are 13 campsites, but there is no drinking water nearby.

9   **TOLSONA RIVER WAYSIDE** is on the south side of the road 155 miles south of Tok and about 15 miles past Glennallen. There are 5 campsites. No drinking water, but there is water nearby that can be boiled.

10   **LAKE LOUISE CAMPGROUND** is a very nice spot about 18 miles up a side road to the north of the highway that goes off 160 miles from Tok. It has 5 campsites and a boat ramp.

11   **LITTLE NELCHINA WAYSIDE** is by the Little Nelchina River near the bridge where the highway crosses it, 190 miles from Tok. There are 6 places.

12   **MANTANUSKA GLACIER WAYSIDE** is just off the road, on the south side, 227 miles from Tok. The glacier itself is visible from the highway for several miles before the campground is reached. Good views of the glacier can be had by walking south from the campground, and it is a fairly easy hike to the base. There are 6 sites.

13   **LONG LAKE WAYSIDE** is off the road about 243 miles from Tok. The campground is beside the lake and has 8 sites and drinking water.

14   **BONNIE LAKE WAYSIDE** is on a side road which goes off 1½ miles on the north side of the highway 245 miles from Tok. The campground is a very pleasant one with 8 sites. The steep, winding access road should be avoided by those towing trailers and should be approached with care in wet weather.

15   **MANTANUSKA RIVER WAYSIDE** is just off the highway 252 miles from Tok. There are 12 sites and drinking water.

16 **MOOSE CREEK WAYSIDE** is on the creek a little north of the highway near the bridge where the road crosses the creek 274 miles from Tok. There are 8 sites and drinking water.

17 **PALMER MUNICIPAL CAMPGROUND** is located on South Denali Street in the town of Palmer, 285 miles from Tok and about 40 miles outside Anchorage. It has a dumping station and modern plumbing, including showers. There are about 70 sites.

18 **FINGER LAKE CAMPGROUND** is 5 miles west of Palmer on the road to Wasilla (and the Anchorage-Fairbanks Highway). There are 36 sites, a boat ramp, and drinking water.

19 **EKLUTNA BASIN** is a pleasant campground in Chugach State Park on a side road that goes off on the south side of the highway 302 miles from Tok. There are 30 sites along the side of Eklutna Lake, about 10 miles from the highway.

20 **PETERS CREEK WAYSIDE** is located on a side road to the south 307 miles from Tok and just a little past the bridge over the creek. There are 32 sites and drinking water.

21 **EAGLE RIVER CAMPSITE AND PICNIC AREA** is by the river on a short side road that goes off to the south of the highway just past the bridge over the Eagle River and the town of the same name. It is 316 miles from Tok. There are 36 sites and drinking water.

22 **CENTENNIAL CAMPER PARK** is a large facility just outside the city of Anchorage on the south side of the road 323 miles from Tok. It has 120 sites, modern plumbing, a dumping station, and it is operated by the Borough of Anchorage.

23 **RUSSIAN JACK SPRINGS and GOOSE LAKE RECREATION AREA** are city parks which provided a few campsites, but it would not be surprising if camping at these sites were to be stopped. Russian Jack Springs,

with 20 sites and drinking water, is south of the highway coming in from Tok on the Boniface Parkway. For Goose Lake, with 18 sites and drinking water, continue south on the Boniface Parkway past Russian Jack Springs and turn right on East Northern Lights Boulevard. Goose Lake will be on the left.

Campgrounds in the Kenai Peninsula

24   **BIRD CREEK CAMP AND PICNIC SITE** is 25 miles from Anchorage on the Seward Highway. It is part of Chugach State Park, and there are 25 sites.

25   **BEAVER POND, BLACK BEAR, and WILLIWAW CAMPGROUNDS** are quite close together on a side road that leaves the Seward Highway to the east 48 miles from Anchorage and a mile past Portage. (From Portage, the Alaska Railroad provides service through a tunnel to Whittier, on the east side of the Kenai Peninsula. Round trip is about $11 for adults, and connection can be made at the other end with ferries to Valdez. Autos are also carried.) The side road leads 5 miles to a visitors' center at the snout of the Portage Glacier. The campsites themselves are very pleasant. Beaver Pond, with 7 spots, is a little less than 3 miles up the road; Black Bear, with 12 sites, is another ¾ mile; and Williwaw, with 38 places, is ¾ mile beyond that. All have drinking water.

26   **BERTHA CREEK CAMPGROUND** is 61 miles from Anchorage, just past the bridge over the creek. There are 10 campsites and drinking water at this pleasant little campground.

27   **GRANITE CREEK CAMPGROUND** is another 2½ miles along the highway from Bertha Creek, about a mile past the Granite Creek Fireguard Station. It has 17 sites and drinking water.

28   **PORCUPINE CAMPGROUND** is near the town of Hope, which is located on a side road that leaves the

main Seward Highway about 70 miles from Anchorage. Hope is about 16 miles along this road. The campground is along the primary side road a little over a mile past the access road to Hope itself. The campground is at a nice place on the south side of Turnagain Arm with lots of possibilities for short walks. This is also the takeoff point for the Resurrection Pass Trail and the western variation discussed in the chapter on backpacking.

29   **TENDERFOOT CREEK CAMPGROUND** is on a short side road to the east by Summit Lake. A pleasant campground with 27 sites and drinking water.

30   **TERN LAKE CAMPGROUND** is a little less than 90 miles from Anchorage and about 2 miles toward Seward from the junction with the Sterling Highway to Kenai, Soldotna, and Homer. This is a good place to see arctic terns, which make annual migrations of about 27,000 miles between the arctic and the antarctic. The campground has 21 sites and drinking water.

31   **TRAIL RIVER CAMPGROUND** is a large facility near Kenai Lake. It is on a side road that goes off to the west of the highway 102 miles from Anchorage and 15 miles from the Sterling Highway cutoff. The side road is a little over a mile long. There are 97 sites with modern plumbing.

32   **PTARMIGAN CREEK CAMPGROUND** is a smaller facility a mile down the highway from the access road to Trail River. There are 16 sites with drinking water, and there is a pleasant trail up the creek to Ptarmigan Lake.

33   **PRIMROSE LANDING CAMPGROUND** is also on Kenai Lake, 109 miles from Anchorage. The access road goes off the highway to the west just after crossing the Snow River on two separate bridges. There are 6 sites, a boat ramp, and drinking water.

34   **SEWARD SMALL BOAT HARBOR, FIRST LAKE CAMPGROUND, and SEWARD HIGHWAY**

CAMPGROUND provide camping facilities at the town of Seward, 125 miles from Anchorage. The Seward Highway Campground is on the right before one gets to the main part of town, a little after the bridge over the Resurrection River and the airport turnoff. It has 22 sites and drinking water. The other main campground is near the Small Boat Harbor on the left side of the road as you enter town. It has 76 sites, a dumping station, and modern plumbing. Tiny First Lake has 5 spots.

35 **QUARTZ CREEK CAMPGROUND** is the first one along the Sterling Highway, after it turns off the Seward Highway 89 miles from Anchorage. It is a little way down the Quartz Creek side road which goes off 7 miles from the junction. There are 23 sites, a boat ramp, and drinking water. The campground is situated at the west end of Kenai Lake.

36 **CRESCENT CREEK CAMPGROUND** is a little more than 2 miles farther along the Quartz Creek access road. Watch for signs, since there are many cabins on Forest Service land along this road and the junctions can be confusing. There are 9 sites and drinking water, and a trail leads to Crescent Lake.

37 **COOPER CREEK CAMPGROUND** is located near the creek and the bridge where the highway crosses it 13 miles past the Seward Highway junction. The campground stretches on both sides of the highway and has 19 sites and drinking water.

38 **RUSSIAN RIVER CAMPGROUND** is near Cooper Landing, a little over 17 miles from the Seward Highway junction. There are two campgrounds on opposite sides of the river, with about 150 places. This is a primary salmon fishing site and is very crowded in season (best determined by a current fishing regulations pamphlet, available in any sporting goods store in Alaska). Drinking water is available.

39 **HIDDEN LAKE** (44 sites), **UPPER SKILAK LAKE** (8

sites), **LOWER OHMER LAKE** (8 sites), **ENGINEER LAKE** (3 sites), **LOWER SKILAK LAKE** (6 sites), **and BOTTINENTNIN LAKE** (2 sites) **CAMPGROUNDS** are all located on an 18-mile-long side road which leaves the main highway a little over 20 miles from the Seward Highway junction and rejoins it 17 miles farther on. The side road is called the Skilak Road. The campsites are located in the order mentioned. Hidden Lake and Skilak have drinking water.

40   **KELLY LAKE, PETERSEN LAKE, and WATSON LAKE CAMPGROUNDS** are located on the main highway where it is paralleled by the Skilak Lake Road. The side road to Kelly and Petersen Lakes goes south ½ mile a little over 31 miles from the Seward Highway junction. Watson Lake Campground is 3 miles farther along the main road. Kelly has 5 sites, and each of the other two has 4.

41   **DOLLY VARDEN LAKE, RAINBOW LAKE, and SWANSON RIVER CAMPGROUNDS** are all located on the Swanson River Road which goes off the highway 47 miles from the Seward Highway junction, just before the village of Sterling. Dolly Varden Lake, with 10 sites and drinking water, is 14 miles up the road; Rainbow Lake, with 5 sites, is 16 miles; and Swanson River, with 6 sites, is 18 miles from the main road. This road is also the access route for the Swan Lake and Swanson River Canoe Trail.

42   **CAPTAIN COOK STATE PARK** is located at the end of the North Kenai Road, which runs north of the rapidly growing town of Kenai. This park will be expanded and will contain several campgrounds, but there are currently 60 sites some 26 miles north of town. In the town itself **KENAI MUNICIPAL PARK** has 30 sites, intended mainly for vehicle campers.

43   **SWIFT WATER CAMPGROUND** is on a short side road going off as one enters the town of Soldotna. There are 30 spaces and a boat ramp. The **SOLDOTNA PARK CAMPGROUND** is reached by turning left on the Sterling Highway at the wye where the Kenai Road branches off and then turning right just after the Kenai River bridge. There are 30 sites and drinking water. A road continues along the beach here through the little town of Kasilof (Kalifonsky Beach Road) and rejoins the Sterling 12 miles to the south.

44 **KASILOF RIVER WAYSIDE** is near the bridge over the river, 15 miles south of the junction where a side road goes off to Kenai (160 miles from Anchorage; 71 miles from the Seward Highway junction). There are 10 sites and drinking water.

45 **JOHNSON LAKE WAYSIDE** is on a side road to the east a mile past the Kasilof River bridge and campground. There are 20 sites and a boat ramp.

46 **TUSTUMENA CAMPGROUND** is 6 miles past Johnson Lake Campground up the same side road. It has 10 sites, drinking water, and a boat ramp.

47 **NINILCHIK WAYSIDE**, near the town of the same name, west of the post office, 41 miles south of the junction with the Kenai Road. The view across Cook Inlet is spectacular. There are 15 sites.

48 **STARISKI WAYSIDE** is 17 miles south of Ninilchik on the Sterling Highway (58 miles from the Kenai junction and 22 miles north of Homer). It is on headlands above Cook Inlet, and one can walk down trails to the beach. There are 12 sites.

49 **ANCHOR RIVER WAYSIDE**, beside the river and a little beyond the bridge where the highway crosses, is about 10 miles south of Stariski Wayside. There are 7 sites.

50 **HOMER FAIRGROUNDS** is a city campground on the left side of the highway as one enters town. It has 15 sites and drinking water. Camping is also permitted on the **HOMER SPIT,** which juts out into the bay, both on public land and in private campgrounds.

Commercially operated campgrounds are available on the Kenai Peninsula in Seward, Cooper Landing, Sterling, Soldotna, Anchor Point, and Homer, and on the Hope side road and the Seward Highway 103 miles from Anchorage.

Campgrounds on the Anchorage-Fairbanks Highway

51 **ROCKY LAKE WAYSIDE and BIG LAKE WAYSIDES** are located off the Anchorage-Fairbanks highway after it turns north from the road leading to Tok (Glenn Highway), some 35 miles out of Anchorage a little before Palmer. The route to Fairbanks here goes to Wasilla and Willow. Wasilla is passed after 7 miles. The side road to the campgrounds turns off 17 miles from the junction. There is a fork 4 miles from the highway, and the right-hand branch goes 2 miles to Big Lake East Wayside, with 14 sites, a boat ramp, and drinking water. The left branch leads to Big Lake South Wayside, 1½ miles from the junction, with 13 sites, a boat ramp, and drinking water; and Rocky Lake about 4 miles away, with 10 sites, a boat ramp, and drinking water. There are also other lakes and numerous cabins in this area. The roads can be a little confusing, particularly at night.

52 **NANCY LAKE WAYSIDE** is near the highway 32 miles from the Glenn Highway junction. There are 30 sites, a boat ramp, and drinking water.

53 **WILLOW CREEK WAYSIDE** is a little beyond the town of Willow, which is 34 miles from the Glenn Highway junction. There are 17 sites.

McKinley National Park

The entrance to McKinley National Park is a little over 200 miles from the junction with the Glenn Highway (235 miles from Anchorage, 120 from Fairbanks). During most of the season (the road is open roughly from the second or third week in June until late

Here the road into McKinley National Park cuts across Polychrome Pass. Take the shuttle bus if mountain roads make you a nervous driver.

September, depending on snow conditions), cars are allowed to drive the park road only to reach assigned campgrounds. General travel in the park is by shuttle buses, which run regularly from park headquarters to the end of the road near Wonder Lake. Cars must stop at park headquarters to make campground reservations. The campgrounds in the park are listed below. No gas is available beyond the entrance.

54 **RILEY CREEK and MORINO CAMPGROUNDS** are near the entrance to the park and have a total of 112 spaces, most at Riley Creek, which also has modern plumbing.

55 **SAVAGE RIVER CAMPGROUND** is 12 miles from the entrance station. It has 24 spaces and modern plumbing.

56 **SANCTUARY RIVER CAMPGROUND** is 22 miles from the entrance station and has 7 spaces.

57 **TEKLANIKA RIVER CAMPGROUND** is 29 miles from the entrance station. It has 35 sites and drinking water.

58 **IGLOO CREEK CAMPGROUND** is 34 miles from the entrance station and has 7 sites.

59 **WONDER LAKE CAMPGROUND** is 84 miles from the entrance station. There is modern plumbing, and there are 23 spaces.

Commercially operated campgrounds on the Anchorage-Fairbanks highway are located at the town of Willow, at McKinley Park, near the entrance road to the park, and at spots 80, 254, and 255 miles from the Glenn Highway junction (242, 69, and 68 miles from Fairbanks).

Campgrounds North of Fairbanks

One can drive north from Fairbanks to several small communities and some pleasant country. The main roads are the Steese Highway, which leads to Circle, currently the farthest north one can drive in the U.S. and Canada, and the Elliott Highway to Livengood and Manley Hot Springs. The two run together for about 10 miles north of Fairbanks, then the Elliott turns off to the west and the Steese goes northeast.

60 **TOLOVANA RIVER CAMPGROUND** is 57 miles along the Elliott Highway from the junction mentioned above. There are 6 sites.

61 **MANLEY HOT SPRINGS PARK** is a little campground and picnic area maintained by local residents of that village. There are 3 sites.

62 **CHATANIKA RIVER WAYSIDE** is a very pleasant campground northwest of the road just after one crosses the bridge over the river, 28 miles along the Steese Highway past the Elliott Highway junction. There are 28 sites and drinking water.

63   **BEDROCK CREEK CAMPGROUND** is on the north-west side of the road 109 miles from the junction. It has 5 sites.

64   **KETCHEM CREEK CAMPGROUND** is off the Steese Highway on the side road that goes off to Circle Hot Springs 117 miles from the Elliott Highway junction. The campground is 7 miles down the side road and has 8 sites. There is also camping at the private campground at Circle Hot Springs Resort, another 1½ miles along the side road.

65   **CIRCLE CITY CAMPGROUND** is a small facility operated by the village at the end of the Steese Highway. It has 4 spaces and drinking water.

Campgrounds Along the Richardson and Denali Highways

The Richardson Highway leaves the road from Tok to Fairbanks and runs south, joining the Tok-Anchorage road for a few miles and then continuing south to Valdez, a port on the Gulf of Alaska. The Denali Highway is a beautiful drive connecting the Richardson Highway with McKinley Park and the Anchorage-Fairbanks road to the west. Until a few years ago, the Denali Highway was the only way to drive to McKinley National Park. The Richardson Highway leaves the Alcan at Delta Junction, milepost 1422. Mileposts on the Richardson Highway begin at Valdez and reach Delta Junction at milepost 266. (Actually, Valdez is 4 miles farther than the mileposts indicate, since the original city was destroyed in the 1964 earthquake and was rebuilt at a new site.)

66   **DONNELLY CREEK WAYSIDE** is on the west side of the highway near milepost 238, 28 miles south of Delta Junction. There are 12 sites.

67   **FIELDING LAKE CAMPGROUND,** on a side road to the west near milepost 201, is a nice campground a little over a mile down the side road with 7 sites.

68 **PAXSON LAKE WAYSIDE** is a small and pleasant campground 5 miles south of the junction with the Denali Highway at Paxson, between mileposts 179 and 180. There are 3 spots near the lake.

69 **SOURDOUGH WAYSIDE** is near milepost 147. There are 6 sites.

70 **LIBERTY FALLS WAYSIDE** is located on the Edgerton Highway, a side road leading east from the Richardson Highway near milepost 83 to the village of Chitina and beyond. The campground is a beautiful spot just off the road some 24 miles from the Richardson Highway. There are 6 sites.

71 **SQUIRREL CREEK WAYSIDE** is between mileposts 79 and 80 on the Richardson Highway, near the bridge over the creek. It has 7 places.

72 **LITTLE TONSINA WAYSIDE**, at milepost 65, has 6 campsites.

73 **WORTHINGTON GLACIER WAYSIDE** is on a short side road to the west just south of milepost 29. It is an interesting spot, since it is near the snout of the glacier, but those not equipped for chilly weather may find the campground cold. There are 6 sites.

74 **BLUEBERRY LAKE WAYSIDE**, at milepost 23, has 6 places.

75 **VALDEZ GLACIER ROAD WAYSIDE** is on the side road which leaves the highway between mileposts 3 and 4 and goes to the Valdez Glacier. The campground is 2 miles up the side road and has 40 sites.

76 **CABIN LAKE CAMPGROUND** is near the town of Cordova which is reached by air or by ferry from Valdez or Whittier (itself reached by the train from Portage). It is thus a little difficult of access unless you bring a car on the ferry. The campground is on a side road that goes north from the road to the airport; it is about 2½ miles from the airport, which is about 12 miles southeast of town. There are 12 campsites.

A visitor to McKinley National Park reads one of the signs explaining the natural history of the vast expanses of tundra that make up most of the park.

77 **DENALI CAMPGROUND** is 22 miles west of Paxson on the Denali Highway to McKinley National Park and the Anchorage-Fairbanks highway. It is an attractive spot a little way from the main road on the north side. There are 12 places.

78 **BRUSHKANA CAMPGROUND** is a little over 104 miles west of Paxson. It has 12 places.

Commercial campgrounds are operated along the Richardson Highway at Copper Center, Paxson, Valdez, and milepost 93.

4

Getting to the North by air is the least interesting way to make the trip, but it is much more economical of time. Perhaps the most important objection to taking an airplane to Alaska or the Yukon is that it robs one of the feeling of great space and remoteness. Air travel deprives the visitor of his sense of dimension and perspective.

There are some very good reasons for travel by air, however. The most important is that if you have limited time you will be able to spend all of it doing what you want to do. For a backpacker, for example, a two-week trip to McKinley Park by car would be a waste of time, even if he managed to get there. He would have to drive the Alcan in such a hurry that its attractions would be ignored, and no time would be left for hiking in the park. On the other hand, air travel will enable him to spend almost his entire vacation actually walking on the tundra below the Alaska Range, a prospect to make any devoted backcountry traveler turn green with envy. For a person traveling alone, air travel may well turn out to be cheaper than a trip by car. For anyone, air and other public transportation at least have the virtue of predictability both in terms of time and expense. There is no worry about having one's car break down in the middle of the Alcan, losing precious days and having one's vacation suddenly cost another $500. Finally, wear and tear on vehicles and nerves are greatly reduced.

For short vacations, air travel is definitely recommended.

One or two objectives should be chosen, so that two or three weeks can be spent savoring particular areas, whether by backpacking, canoe travel, camping on the shore of a wilderness lake, or staying in a remote Forest Service cabin. Hopping around and trying to see everything on a short vacation is usually a waste of time.

For those having a little more leisure, but not enough for driving, the best combination is probably to take the ferry system north, travel on into the Yukon or the main part of Alaska by bus or train, and return by air, unless bad weather on the trip up makes one want to try another ferry trip back.

Air Service to Alaska and the Yukon

There are many types of air service to even the smallest villages in the Yukon, Alaska, and northern British Columbia, far more than one would expect to much larger population centers in, say, Kansas or New England. The North depends heavily on aircraft to link widely separated settlements. Thus, the tourist can easily get air service almost anywhere he likes.

The ways of getting to Alaska and the Yukon by air include charter flights, package tours, and regularly scheduled airline service. Charter flights are the most economical, provided that they can be arranged and that they suit your schedule. Regulations generally require that everyone taking a charter flight have been a member of the sponsoring organization for a particular length of time. Trips to Alaska sponsored by hiking and mountaineering clubs may include a charter flight with the option of continuing with the group or going out on your own.

Tours may be good for people who want much of their trip prearranged. Some are more flexible than others, allowing

Camping by Kluane Lake. Stoves like this one are provided at all territorial campgrounds in the Yukon, but carry an ax for splitting large chunks if you want to be able to make use of the stoves.

various optional trips, usually at additional cost. Unfortunately, commercially run tours are rarely oriented toward those interested in camping or wilderness travel.

Unless you are lucky enough to find a charter or a tour that works into your plans, you will probably take a commercial scheduled airline. If you want to fly as economically as possible, you should check rates and schedules carefully. Ticket and travel agents often do not charge the cheapest applicable rates, so it always pays to check with several agents. Find out whether a different schedule would allow you to fly under a cheaper plan. If you are going to Alaska, investigate the possibility of flying via Canada, since you will not only have the opportunity to visit more places this way, but you may be able to save money; international flight rates are generally cheaper than domestic ones. Thus, from some

United States cities, it may be cheaper to fly first to Canada and to make connections through Whitehorse.

From the contiguous United States, flights to various Alaskan cities are made by Alaska Airlines, Pan American World Airways, Northwest Orient Airlines, and Western Airlines. Various international airlines make flights from other countries. Canadian Pacific Air flies to Whitehorse in the Yukon Territory from many Canadian cities, and service between Whitehorse and Alaskan cities is provided by Wien Air Alaska.

Within the Yukon Territory, regularly scheduled service is provided from Whitehorse to Dawson City, Mayo, Clinto Creek, Old Crow, Faro, and Ross River by Northward Aviation.

There are a host of small airlines offering service between virtually all Alaskan towns. The largest are Alaska Airlines and Wien Air Alaska. The Alaska division of tourism will provide information on request about both scheduled and private service between any points in which you are interested.

5

Car Camping

Camping near roadways in Alaska and northern Canada can be the basis of a very enjoyable family vacation or the cause of considerable misery, depending on your preparation and luck. There are many beautiful campgrounds in the North, but the traveler will be making a grave error if he expects the kind of outdoor motel, complete with swimming pool, amusement park, and piped utilities, that has become common in the "lower forty-eight." There are a few private campgrounds of this type in Alaska, but they are the exception. The best campsites are often the most primitive, in any case, so the visitor should be prepared to camp without modern amenities. In general, outhouses are provided, and drinking water is available at about half the public areas.

Campers in the North will usually be happiest with a reasonably sturdy and reliable vehicle, a matter which has been discussed earlier. Those with smaller and more maneuverable cars and trucks will have a greater range of possibilities available, since they will be able to negotiate roads that will stop large camping machines and trailers. Vehicles with four-wheel drive, though hardly necessary, have a considerable advantage on dirt roads, particularly during spring thaw or long periods of rain. Many campers who like to drive into areas with poor roads find that a few extra tools, such as a come-along winch and a tow chain, cable, or rope, provide additional peace of mind.

Preparation is the key to enjoyable car camping in the

Here a pickup camper stops for the night at a spot ideal for a few hours of fishing or contemplation.

north, preparation in terms of equipment, mental attitude, time, and planning. Equipment must be reliable and suitable to the conditions. Campers should be prepared for some mediocre campsites as well as beautiful ones, particularly driving to Alaska. Distances in the North are great, travel may be slow, and attempts to cover too much ground in too little time usually result in unenjoyable trips. Supplies and repairs are likely to be hard to get and expensive when they are available, so careful planning is essential.

Trailers, Pickup Campers, and Camping Machines

The main roads in Alaska are paved, and the roads into most maintained campgrounds are quite adequate, so there are no real difficulties involved for owners of camping vehicles who want to take them to Alaska. Travel on the Alcan Highway has already been discussed. Most drivers who come to grief have overloaded their vehicles or tried to drive too fast. Camping vehicles are generally equipped with fairly soft springs and axles of moderate strength, and they can only hit so many chuckholes at fifty or sixty miles per hour before something gives way.

Drivers of heavy vehicles should also beware of soft shoulders, particularly after long periods of rain. Roads into established campgrounds generally have a good gravel base, and adequate clearance and turning space, but in case of any doubts, it is wise to walk in first and check, particularly if you have a large vehicle, are towing a heavy trailer, or if the ground is very wet.

Driving long distances on gravel roads tends to shake a vehicle more than one might think. Some screwed connections are bound to be shaken loose occasionally, so owners of camping vehicles should take care to check bottled or piped gas connections. Don't enter the camper with lighted cigarettes or lanterns in hand until you've checked for gas.

Most prepared campgrounds have level pads for campers on wheels, but in some less developed areas, owners of camping machines will have to make do. Piped-in hookups are generally nonexistent, except at a few commercially run campgrounds near the larger cities. Dumping stations are generally found only in towns and at some service stations, but in off seasons—early in spring and late in fall—expect many information centers and dumping stations to be closed. If you are spending a lot of time away from population centers, or if you are traveling off-season, plan to make use of service station facilities, pit toilets, and the like, at least some of the time. *Do not dump your holding tank except in proper disposal areas.* Sanitation is a particular problem in the North,

A sunny morning may be a time for a peaceful cup of coffee and airing out the bedding.

where biological breakdown of waste is slow and where the ground is often frozen just below the surface, preventing the soil from absorbing waste material.

Tents

Be sure that your tent is sturdy, well-made, and in good repair before packing it up. It should be able to shed rain for long periods, since even interior regions sometimes get precipitation for days on end during the camping season, and coastal areas are notoriously damp. Cheap tents that will not stand up well to rain and hard wind for weeks at a time are generally not well-suited to the kind of extended camping that is likely on your Alaska trip.

Some thought should also be given to the size of the tent when you plan your trip. A small backpacking tent is versatile and easy to pitch, but it can be miserably cramped during long periods of rain. Light, bright colors are usually much more bearable during wet spells than dark fabrics that transmit little light. If a small tent is used, an extra tarp or fly of some kind may be taken to pitch over an eating area for extra living space.

Many campgrounds are now designed primarily for vehicles rather than tents, so that the camper will sometimes be forced to pitch his tent on a gravel pad. Foam pads, air mattresses, or cots should be carried to make sleeping in such circumstances comfortable. Since regular stakes do not work well on this type of surface, it is best also to carry a set of spikes and a hammer with which to drive them. Lengths of parachute cord will allow easy use of trees, bushes, and rocks for anchoring.

Stoves and Fires

Campers who customarily use stoves will not need to make any significant changes in their cooking habits while camping in the North. Enough fuel should be carried to last until the next convenient resupply point, but naphtha fuel and propane are usually easy to obtain in population centers and at many service stations. If you use a stove that requires special cartridges, you had best take enough fuel to last the whole trip.

Fires are always pleasant in camp, of course, and you will find wood supplied in many campgrounds in British Columbia, Alaska, and the Yukon. Several cautions are necessary, however. *Please, be very careful with fire in the North.* The population in most regions is far too small to allow fighting forest fires that do not directly threaten a settlement. A fire started by a careless camper will probably burn thousands or hundreds of thousands of acres of forest before being put out by storms. There is no excuse for carelessness with fire anywhere, but in the North, the damage caused by such negligence is likely to be far greater than in more populated areas, where reforestation is quicker.

Stoves or fireplaces should be used wherever they are provided, and it is usually illegal to build an open fire rather than use the fireplace. Even at campsites with stoves or grates, the camper should look carefully at the surrounding ground, the dryness of the forest, and the wind conditions before building a fire. Wind-carried sparks can start a major blaze quickly when the woods are dry. Never leave a fire going when you go away from your camp, even when you think you will only be gone for a half hour or so. Never build fires on bogs, forest humus, or other vegetable matter; sparks can smolder deep below the surface for weeks before breaking out into flame long after you are gone. The need to be careful with cigarettes and matches should be obvious, but apparently it still is not to many people.

When wood is provided in public campgrounds, it often is sawed from logs into chunks a few feet long. This is a definite advantage when the weather has been rainy for extended periods, since often there is still dry wood at the centers of the larger chunks, but you will find this wood impossible to use unless you carry tools for splitting it. Bring an ax if you want fires. For those unfamiliar with the techniques of splitting, a few tips are given in the box.

Kindling to get the fire going can easily be split from the chunks provided, but when there are long spells of wet weather, it is easier to dry some kindling out each time you have a fire and carry it in the car or keep it in the tent until the next fire-building time. Once the fire is going well, particularly if you are using one of the stoves provided at many campgrounds, it will be easy enough to burn larger and wetter pieces. In wet weather, chemical fire starters speed up fire building. A candle held under kindling serves the same purpose.

If you want fires where wood is not provided, it is best to stop and pick up dead wood before reaching camp, either from deadfall or in a fire-kill area. Wood lying on the ground may be scarce around campgrounds. Please don't chop down standing trees, alive or dead, near campgrounds. A bow saw is useful for sawing chunks from fallen logs.

Outside of organized campgrounds, you must have a permit to build fires in the Yukon and British Columbia. You can obtain them from the Forest Service or Royal Canadian Mounted Police stations.

Other Cooking Equipment

Since you will probably be camping for some time on your Alaska trip, it will be best to bring pots that are fairly heavy and of adequate size, whether they are special camping cookware or are appropriated from kitchen use. Pans that will pack compactly are nice, but if they are made of thin aluminum, food will burn too easily and too often. Be sure to carry a heavy frying pan, particularly if you plan to fish and to fry your catch. Lightweight pots are a necessity for the backpacker, but the extra difficulty they cause can be avoided when car camping. If you plan to backpack also, carry a couple of larger and heavier pans to supplement your regular backpacking cook kit. Teflon coating, while hardly essential, makes cleanup easier. If you are cooking over fires, carry each pan in a plastic bag so that you will not have to clean soot off the outside after every meal.

If you want to speed up cooking and make the use of regular staples such as rice and beans more practical, consider taking a pressure cooker. A lot of inexpensive camp meals can be prepared easily and quickly this way.

Don't neglect adequate hot pan holders, a large spoon and a spatula, and enough pot scrubbers. A biodegradable soap is better than detergent, since it presents less of a disposal problem.

Finding a Campsite

Besides campsites listed in chapter 11, there are literally thousands of beautiful camping spots throughout the North, many of them providing a near paradise for the outdoor enthusiast. There are rushing streams, lakes beyond counting, and spectacular mountain backdrops. However, there are also hundreds of miles of bogs, swampy tundra, and steep, dense forests. The weary traveler is likely to find that many areas have few suitable campsites other than prepared roadside stops, particularly for the car camper.

For these reasons, until you become familiar with a particular area, it is best to plan to use designated camping sites. Otherwise, you may end by being happy to find a gravel turnout in which to spend the night.

All the campgrounds available in northern British Columbia, the Yukon, and Alaska at the time of writing are listed in this book, though others may open later. Commercially operated campgrounds open and close frequently, and there may also be some unintentional errors of omission. In spring and fall, some campgrounds may be closed, and it is well to check in advance.

British Columbia's policy in the last few years has been to operate small numbers of large, well-maintained, and beautifully situated public campgrounds. They are practically ideal for the motorized camper, with broad, well-graded roads and impeccably level gravel pads. The tenter may sometimes have

Morning at a late fall camp in Alaska. The shrubs have lost many of their leaves, and snows are not far away, but the brisk mornings and autumn colors compensate the late season camper.

harsh words to say about the surfacing of the sites, but no one is likely to quarrel about the loveliness of the surroundings. The small number of sites causes occasional crowding problems, however, and the distance between campgrounds is often considerable. British Columbia's campgrounds are often closed after 10 P.M., so you may have to stop earlier than you would like to avoid getting caught out on the road. The nightly fee per site in British Columbia's provincial campgrounds is $2–$3 from May 1 to mid-September. Campgrounds along the various roads leading to Alaska and the ferry routes are listed in appropriate chapters.

The Yukon has smaller campgrounds spaced more frequently than those in British Columbia. The campsites in the Yukon are particularly convenient for travelers, though they vary a good deal in scenic attractions and facilities. Most are provided with wood, stoves, and a central cookhouse that can be a blessing in prolonged wet or cold weather. The stoves are a model of economy and efficiency; they are made from used oil drums. You pay an annual fee of $3 for use of the public campgrounds in the Yukon, a real bargain. Sleeping in the central cookhouses is prohibited.

Alaska has public campgrounds run under several government auspices: State of Alaska, United States Forest Service, Bureau of Land Management, and United States Park Service. The annual permit fee for use of Alaska state parks and waysides is $10. In general, there are no fees charged for use of federal campground facilities, except for Forest Service cabins and national park facilities. National park entrance fees and some other fees at Federal facilities are covered with a Golden Eagle card, an annual permit which can be purchased for $10 at any national park.

Clothing

No really specialized clothing is required for camping in normal seasons in the North. Days are generally warm and nights are cool enough to often persuade one to put on a hat, wool sweater, and shell parka. In spring and fall, evening temperatures may often drop below freezing, but the same sort of clothing that is suitable for camping in the Colorado Rockies or in northern Maine at the same time of year is adequate.

Comfortable, functional clothes are always most suitable for extended camping trips, and these are more satisfactory if they are easily washed and don't show dirt too quickly. Some wool clothing is useful on cool nights, particularly in wet weather. Clothes that don't require ironing make laundering easier.

Sturdy hiking boots and heavy wool socks are essential if you plan to stray far from your car. Boots suitable for wet muddy conditions are needed in some areas and seasons. For trips in the early spring or late summer, some cold weather clothing is advisable, such as long underwear and perhaps a down jacket.

Bedding

Cool nights are common in much of the North, so your sleeping bags or other bedding should be adequate to keep you warm. Your exact needs will depend on whether you will be sleeping in a vehicle, in a tent, or outdoors, but in the summer you should plan for occasional nighttime temperatures in the forties. In spring or fall, you should be ready for some freezing nights. Try to choose bedding that will also allow adequate ventilation when the temperatures are warmer, as they often will be.

Tent campers should have good foam pads or air mattresses, which provide for more comfortable nights and greatly increase the warmth of sleeping bags. Most people find that foam pads around two inches thick make the most comfortable beds. They are easier to get used to than air mattresses and are warmer. Pads three inches thick make true luxury accommodations. Remember that some campsites will require sleeping on packed gravel surfaces, which are most uncomfortable without some sort of ground bed.

Air out your bedding whenever you have the chance. Bedding that has become damp from atmospheric moisture or perspiration is cold and uncomfortable, so hang your sleeping bags out in the sun while you are doing other camp chores.

Insects

The North is known for the number and appetite of its bugs. At some times and places the insects of the North live up to their reputation, but things are not always nearly as bad as legend would suggest. Frequently, the camper in Alaska will have less trouble with mosquitos and other pests than he would at home. The insect problem is at its worst around the extensive boggy areas that occur in much of the North, particularly in permafrost regions, but severity varies from year to year, as well as with the season, amount of wind, and so forth.

Insects are much less of a problem these days. Modern repellents are much more offensive to insects and much less so to people than the concoctions that were available a few years ago. *Take plenty of a good repellent along.* (Department of Agriculture studies show the most effective active ingredient to be N,N-diethyl-metatoluamide. The higher the percentage of active ingredient, the better.) Then, when bugs start biting, don't wait too long to use the repellent. Aerosols are more expensive and less concentrated, but they are good for treating clothing.

A tent with mosquito netting which is tight at all points will help a good deal when insects are bad, except when the problem is with small biting gnats called no-see-ums, which go right through the netting. For those who like to sleep out under the stars, a mosquito bar provides similar protection. This is a large section of netting that can be draped over the sleeping bag, with some arrangement for holding it away from the face.

Animals

Avoid leaving food, especially smelly food, out in the open, where it will be sure to tempt the local animal population.

The simplest way to avoid having your provisions pilfered is to lock them in the car before retiring or going fishing. People rarely have problems with bears if they avoid confrontations, do not leave food lying around, and do not feed wild animals. Both the animals and their human observers are better off if the animals do not become dependent on people for food. In the case of small animals, the results of feeding are often sad; large animals like bears may become dangerous if their source of tourist-borne food is suddenly removed, or if people begin to assume they are tame.

Most scavenging bears are black bears (whether they are black or brown). They are rarely dangerous, unless the camper becomes casual about them or gets between a mother and her cub. A black bear molesting a camp can often be shouted away with some caution and from a safe distance. Grizzlies, on the other hand, are considerably more dangerous and should be given a very wide berth. They can easily be distinguished by the large humps over their shoulders. Grizzlies are likely to avoid people in most cases and today are rarely seen near most roads, except in parks where they are protected.

Moose should also be given a wide berth. Like most wild animals they are dangerous only when they feel challenged or cornered, but in those circumstances they can be formidable animals. In general, those seeing large animals in the North should feel fortunate indeed. None of these animals present any danger to the observer, if some respect for their wild state is observed. An animal will usually only feel threatened if a person gets between it and its young, approaches too closely, is blocking a path, or provokes the animal.

6

Backpacking in the North

The vast wilderness areas of Alaska, the Yukon, and northern British Columbia are a paradise for the backpacker, presenting virtually infinite scope and variety. The paradise is an unfamiliar one, though. There are a number of developed trails that have easy road access, the circumstance that most backpackers from the "lower forty-eight" are familiar with. In fact, these trails go through fine country and are well worth traveling. Most of the North, however, is true wilderness, trackless, remote, difficult to get to, and often very hard to get through. There are no well-worn trails, no Forest Service signs, and usually no one to get the overconfident neophyte out of trouble. Route finding must be done with map, compass, and seat of the pants. Maps are not always reliable. Terrain may provide easy walking, allowing progress of fifteen miles a day, or the going may be so hard that strong and experienced wilderness travelers fight desperately to make a mile or two.

All this is simply to say that true wilderness travel needs to be taken seriously and requires careful planning. Bad preparation will spoil a trip and may be dangerous as well. Hikers who are landed by float plane and left for a month to make their way to a prearranged rendezvous are very much on their own. Any item of equipment that is forgotten will have to be done without.

General Planning

Naturally, the first consideration in planning a trip will be the location. The time of year is important in anticipating the conditions you might meet. You should consider the difficulty and discomfort you are willing to undergo as well as the scenery you are looking for. The spectacular beauty of the Coast Ranges has a grandeur and ruggedness that can be found nowhere else, but it cannot be viewed from easy walks along the hillsides. Dense, steep forests extend practically to the edge of permanent snow, and rain lasts for weeks on end. Those who want more reasonable walking conditions will be obliged to turn a bit farther inland.

Similarly, the choice of seasons will often make a vast difference. On the tundra, and in other boggy areas, for example, a trip late in the season will bring the risk of cold snaps and some snow, but it will also avoid insects, permit hiking in the driest time of the year other than winter, and allow viewing both vegetation and wildlife at a particularly interesting stage of the yearly cycle. Flashlights can be dispensed with in late June; insect repellent cannot. A particular river crossing may be trivial before the spring breakup and impossible afterwards.

The visitor to the wilderness will have to consider the general terrain and vegetation where he wants to go, whether there are trails and how good they are likely to be, what conditions of temperature and rainfall are to be expected, what extremes need to be prepared for, the distance to be covered and the daily progress that might be expected, and finally, barriers that may have to be passed, such as rivers, mountains, or lakes.

Except in the case of trips about which detailed information is available, from literature or directly from people who have made them before, careful study of the best available topographic maps will be necessary at the most rudimentary planning stages. Most general maps cover far too great an area to give any of the information that will be vital to the foot traveler. Exceptions are trips on established trails or cross-country routes, which may be planned from readily available information. The most detailed topographic maps available should be obtained before actually setting out. For planning trips of your own conception, large-scale topo maps are good for an overview. In Alaska, the 1:250,000 scale maps are good for this purpose, while the 1:63,360 series should be used for detailed planning, when available. Canadian maps are available with similar scales. Write for index maps to determine which one you will need. Most of the trips discussed in this book include a list of the maps needed. Remember to order maps well in advance, since they will sometimes be temporarily out of print. One caution about trails shown on maps of the North: a trail marked as a "winter trail" is almost never suitable for summer use. In heavy snow areas, the trail is likely to go over willow and alder patches covered by snow in winter but almost impassable in summer. In regions of tundra and bog, a winter trail will usually keep to places too wet for heavy vegetation growth, and thus not be suitable for a summer stroll.

Anyone considering a backpacking trip in wilderness areas should also go to great pains to search out information on the region he has in mind, particularly if the trip is to be his first journey to the North. Many routes that might look quite feasible to the neophyte are really virtually impassable in summer. Boggy areas interspersed with tangles of black spruce extend for hundreds of miles and make fine going for moose, but not for backpackers. Study all the available maps closely and read any books you can find on the area. Places marked on maps as marshes or bogs and those where contour

Terrain like this makes for extremely difficult going without a trail. The hillsides are not only steep but heavily forested. Glaciers abound, and stream banks are steep and heavily overgrown, all typical of the coastal mountains.

lines show a large flat region with vague drainage patterns often make very difficult going. Similarly, forested terrain where rainfall is high will be hard to get through without a trail.

Allow plenty of extra food, especially if you are flying in or will be in an area that requires a long walk out. Unexpected delays must always be planned for. Use proven menus that are palatable to all members of the party and are adequate to satisfy their hunger after a day of hard hiking. Long wilderness trips are not good testing grounds for untried rations. If you are using stoves for cooking, be sure to bring adequate fuel. If any time is to be spent on snow, so that water will have to be melted, carry twice the fuel for those days. Take a stove you have used before and can depend on. Carry any spare parts that might be needed, and if you use a butane- or propane-fueled model that requires special cartridges, you had better take enough with you to last the whole trip. (Check shipping regulations on these, if you are going by air.) The cartridges may not be available even in the larger Alaskan towns. Avoid strong-smelling foods, particularly those packed in large containers that are carried over for several meals. Half-used and inadequately sealed peanut butter, sardines, bacon, and the like are excellent lures for bears.

Carry lots of matches in separate waterproof containers and some kind of fire starter; a candle works quite well. If you are using fires, be extremely careful to avoid any possibility of their spreading. In rainy regions, be prepared for wet wood; this may often mean carrying an ax to split chunks, but please leave the places you go as attractive as you found them. On the tundra there may be no wood available, or the few stands that grow might be best left for others to enjoy. If you build fires, use existing fire rings or cover the stones you use with mineral soil, which can later be scattered, leaving the stones unscarred.

Though insects are not always a problem in the North, backpackers who fail to prepare for them may go through an experience so unpleasant they will never forget it. The North has dozens of species of mosquitos, with hatching times carefully spaced so that one can only be sure of missing them in the winter. Carry plenty of the strongest repellent you can buy (the one with the highest percentage of N,N-diethyl-metatoluamide). At times, heavy clothing together with a head net and work gloves is the best answer.

Layers of clothing provide the most versatile combination, including shirt and pants of wool or a wool substitute, a warm hat, and a windbreaker. Several light- and medium-weight shirts and sweaters give more temperature control than one heavy jacket. Carry enough heavy wool socks so that you will normally have a dry pair to change to. Boggy areas are common in most parts of the North, even on the North Slope tundra, which receives little rain, but where standing water is held by the permafrost just below the surface vegetation. Conventional hiking or mountaineering boots are good for most trips, but they should be of reasonable weight and of full leather so that they can be made reasonably resistant to water. Lightweight split leather boots cannot be treated effectively for water repellency. Well-tested and broken-in boots should be taken on any extended wilderness trip. New boots that fall apart or chew up your feet are a definite liability.

Equipment

Tents on long trips receive a lot of wear, and cheap ones are likely to fall apart. In general, nylon tents with a permeable roof and a separate waterproof rain fly have proved best, especially in rainy areas. Waterproof floors, preferably extending partway up the sides, are desirable, as is complete insect screening. Individual insect bars should be carried otherwise. A larger tent makes drying equipment easier during periods of extended rain.

Good sleeping bags will make for a much more comfortable trip. Down bags are standard, though there are some good arguments for the heavier and bulkier bags using synthetic fibers for insulation, since they can be dried much more easily. In any case the bags should be well-made and designed for backpackers, not car campers.

Raingear should be given special attention, particularly for trips in the wetter regions. Plastic items are not durable enough for extended trips, and coated nylon is generally best. No perfect solution has ever been found to keep the hiker and his pack protected from the rain coming down from above without soaking him with the condensed moisture from his body. This is a particular problem with rain in cold weather. The author has found a "foamback" *cagoule* (a long, roomy parka) to be the best answer, together with rain chaps. The foamback has a thin layer of foam bonded to the inside of the waterproof fabric to prevent warm, moist air from the body from coming in direct contact with cold, slick, coated nylon. This greatly reduces condensation. Ponchos also work well, providing there are no strong winds blowing and that brush is not too dense.

First aid kits and repair items should be carefully put together, with individual needs and equipment kept in mind. Good adhesive tape in large quantities is always valuable for patching up people and equipment both. Individuals who have special medical problems that may require unusual care or medication should inform their companions, in case of an emergency. A good knowledge of first aid by all members of the party is only prudent. On an extended wilderness trip, it may be wise to consult a physician about the advisability of carrying some drugs that require prescriptions and getting explicit directions on their use. Examples of such drugs are pain killers and antibiotics. If this course is followed, get a letter describing the drugs from the doctor in case of questions at border crossings.

Water purification tablets may be necessary in many areas where there are human habitations nearby, though drinking water can always be boiled.

Maps, compasses, and thorough familiarity with their use are indispensable for wilderness travel. Compass declination due to the difference between true and magnetic north is very important in this region, since errors can be very large.

If any travel on snow is expected, dark glasses and good sun cream are important to prevent snow-blindness and

Crossing an individual channel of a river. Socks may be taken off, but boots should be worn to protect the feet. The waistbelt of the pack should be unfastened. On a more difficult crossing than this one a staff might be used.

sunburn. Steep snow will require an ice ax and training in its use. It may also require a rope, as glacier travel definitely does. Those planning trips in spring and early summer should expect to find winter conditions still prevailing a few thousand feet up.

Routes

There are quite a few backpacking trips following established trails, though maintenance and marking of these trails will vary considerably. Some that have been set up in the Chugach and Tongass national forests in Alaska will be easy for anyone to follow. Others are old and overgrown use-trails that merely ease the burden of bushwhacking. In most of the

North there are no trails at all, and parties seeking pleasant backpacking trips should choose routes where there is some chance of making progress without having to go through a major struggle for every foot gained. This most commonly means that cross-country trips should be planned in places where the rainfall is not too heavy and where the terrain is hilly enough to provide drainage. Hilly tundra often provides good routes above most of the trees and brush and below the line of permanent snow. For example, hiking in the Peters Hills, above the Susitna River in Alaska, is very pleasant and not particularly difficult, but much of the lower country to the east and south is extremely difficult to get through, due to bogs, brush, and deadfall. The Peters Hills afford a superb view of McKinley when the mountain is clear and can be reached by turning off the Anchorage-Fairbanks Highway on the Peters Creek Road at mile 115. One drives thirty miles or so up a fairly good dirt road, taking the right-hand fork of the road at Peters Creek, nineteen miles in, and passing Petersville in another ten miles. One can begin hiking in another mile or so. The 1:250,000 Talkeetna map shows the area; quad C2 is the small-scale section.

It would, therefore, make much more sense for most parties to plan a cross-country backpack trip of a few weeks in the lower elevations of McKinley National Park or in the Brooks Range than in the trailless areas of the Coast Range or the hills above Juneau or Seward, since the former areas have lots of well-drained hilly tundra, while the latter go directly from glaciers to rain forest and thick alder.

Animals

In some parts of the North you may still see some of the most interesting wildlife in North America. The large mammals, in particular, are one of the major attractions of a trip to Alaska, the Yukon, and northern British Columbia. For the backpacker, however, a reasonable amount of care is necessary to prevent encounters with the larger inhabitants of the wilderness from becoming too close and too exciting.

Bears and moose are the only animals that might pose any danger to the hiker, since they are the only ones which will occasionally fight with a person who is not intentionally attacking them. As with most other wild animals, however, bears and moose will very rarely bother a human unless they are provoked. The best way to avoid unpleasant encounters is to learn how to avoid annoying large animals unintentionally.

One of the dangerous situations that may arise for the backpacker, particularly when he is alone, results when an animal is surprised at close quarters; he or she is startled, just as you are, and may act aggressively, just as humans often do in similar circumstances. This is the main source of danger in encountering moose, who in most situations will avoid people or ignore them. The problem is most likely to occur on forest trails, when the air is still or the wind is blowing against the hiker. One rounds a bend, finds himself face-to-face with a grizzly or a bull moose, and an uncomfortable situation then ensues for both parties.

As with most confrontations, the best solution is avoidance. Bears and moose will do their part if you make sure they know you are around the bend. There are many ways to do this, from whistling, talking, or singing to wearing a bell or other noisemaker attached to your pack or body. All this is unnecessary where visibility is good.

If you do meet a large animal on the trail, talk, yell, and gesture confidently and slowly back out of the way if possible. Get off the track and let the animal pass. Don't turn around and run from a bear unless you've managed to distract him with something else long enough to allow you to climb a tree. Distractions include throwing a hat or article of clothing; the smell may either get the animal to turn around and leave or cause him to attack the clothing, giving you a chance to depart. With moose, simply getting out of the way is usually sufficient. Do not start throwing rocks or sticks at the animal; the trick is to give him a chance to depart without losing face, not to escalate the conflict.

A word to those who insist on carrying guns to protect themselves: if you shoot a bear, you had better kill him with that shot. A shot that does not immediately kill the animal will cause the secretion of enough adrenalin to enable a large grizzly to absorb a hail of bullets afterward and still attack you or escape. If he escapes and lives, hatred of people and possible disabilities may later result in the death of another person as a direct result of your shooting the animal. The fine record of nonviolent encounters between grizzlies and men in places like Katmai National Monument speaks volumes about man-bear relations. In other areas, bears who have learned that men often shoot guns at them tend to be less tolerant of people, a fact that hardly seems mysterious.

The well-known instinct of a mother to protect her young presents another hazard to hikers from moose and bears. Coming upon a moose with a calf or a sow bear with cubs should immediately alert the backpacker to retreat. A mother who would normally be quite peaceable may be very aggressive when she is accompanied by her young. The farther away you get (preferably without turning your back), the less threat you will be. Worse yet is the situation of coming upon the young first; the mother will not be far away, and the last thing you want to do is to get between the mother and the young. A sow can be a considerable distance away, but in my observation, she will normally be downwind of the cubs. Stay far away, because if you should pass downwind of the young bears, you may be suddenly surprised by the sow coming over the hill at incredible speed.

There are virtually limitless possibilities for wilderness backpacking in the North. Here a backpacker views the peaks of the Alaska Range.

Grizzlies are by far the most dangerous animals the backpacker is likely to meet in the North. They are generally larger than their cousins the black bears, but more important, they are far less predictable in their dealings with people. For the great majority of wilderness travelers, the danger is minimal, because most bears would prefer to avoid fights, just as most people would. Occasionally, however, either because the bear is unusual or because he has been inadvertently provoked, a grizzly will attack. The best defense is to climb a tree, if one is available and the victim has time, possibly after tossing a piece of clothing to divert the bear. A grizzly will signal his attack by laying his ears back, so if this occurs, a charge should be anticipated. Cubs are good tree climbers, but mature grizzlies are usually not, though like all rules stated about grizzlies, there have been exceptions to this one.

If no tree is available or there is not enough time to get up one, the only alternative available to the hiker is to fall to the ground, preferably into a hollow, a depression, or a mudhole, face downward with the hands and arms protecting the back of the head and neck. Leave your pack on—it will protect your back, and the bear may bite it instead of you. Try to play dead, while protecting yourself as well as you can. Even attacking bears are normally only interested in removing you as a threat and will soon leave.

Grizzlies are distinguished from black bears not by color, since grizzlies can be black and black bears brown, but by size and shape. The easiest field mark to recognize is the large shoulder hump of the grizzly, the shoulder muscles that enable it to dig for food and help it to propel itself much faster than a man can run.

Food, Campsites, Bears, and Rodents

The two most common causes of bear trouble are completely avoidable: attracting bears with food and camping in the middle of a bear's way. The rules are simple. Don't leave food, especially smelly food, lying around camp. Try to avoid leaving really smelly food out at all. Cosmetics and perfumed soaps also attract bears. Burn your garbage, when possible, as soon as the meal is over, or at least seal it in plastic bags. Hang all foodstuffs on a line between two trees or two rocks, out of a bear's reach, and at least a little way from camp. If there is no way to hang the food, cache it some distance from camp. It would be best to put sealed food that will not smell in a separate cache in this case, so that the risk of losing all your food is lessened. Don't leave fish offal lying around to attract bears. *Never sleep with food in your tent;* a bear may have to go over you to get it.

In wooded areas, the most convenient and attractive spots for sleeping are often along animal tracks, but you would be wise to remember that the grizzly who uses the path every night might regard you and your sleeping bag as undesirable obstructions. Any path or track in a wooded area is probably used by the inhabitants of the forest, including moose and bears, so find another place to bed down.

While you are protecting your food from the bears, give some consideration to rodents as well. Try to make the food inaccessible to them, particularly if you are staying a few days. Put as much food as possible in containers that small animals can't chew into. A busy colony of mice and voles can carry off very large amounts of food in one night, and you don't want to have to start digging up their holes to try to recover your granola when the pilot won't be back for a month.

River and Stream Crossings

When you are planning your trip, give careful consideration to the problem of crossings. Much of the water in the North is quite close to freezing temperatures, and wading through icy torrents is serious business. Swimming far in water of that temperature is out of the question without a diver's wet suit. Rafts require some time to make, and they can only be used on lakes or slow rivers where wood is available. Wading should be undertaken with great care, using some kind of staff on the upstream side as a third leg and moving only one support at a time. Waist straps on packs should be undone so that the loads can be jettisoned in case of a slip. It is generally best to remove one's socks to keep them dry, but to wear the boots to protect the feet and improve footing, particularly since the feet will soon lose their feeling in cold water. Some hikers prefer to carry a pair of sneakers for stream crossings.

Unless a crossing can be made on trees or protruding rocks, the backpacker should pick the widest spot in the river for wading, since it is usually the shallowest and slowest. In braided rivers, those silt-laden glacial streams with many channels, cross at the most braided point, walking up and down to find the shallowest part of each channel. Water coming above the knees is likely to be dangerous if it is at all swift. On dangerous crossings, the lead person should be secured by a line from shore in such a way that the current will carry him toward safe ground. He can set up a hand line for others to use. In deep wilderness trips, the supplies should be distributed so that the loss of any one pack will not be dangerous.

Recommended Trips

For beginners and others wanting a pleasant backpack trip along well-established trails, there are a number of nice trips on the Kenai Peninsula, south of Anchorage, accessible by good roads. One is the Resurrection Pass Trail, which follows the Resurrection Creek and Juneau Creek valleys from the town of Hope, on Turnagain Arm, to Cooper Landing at the end of Kenai Lake. The distance one way is about thirty-six miles. For those who would rather stay in them, there are six Forest Service cabins spaced along the trail. Write to the Chugach National Forest for a map showing the cabin locations and the district lines. Reservations are made with the district rangers and should be made well in advance. The trail is easily found from either end. For an overview, the 1:250,000 Seward map shows the whole route. The detailed topo maps are Seward B8, C7, C8, D7, and D8.

This glacier is one of the many attractions of Stewart Road in British Columbia.

For the more adventurous, there is an excellent parallel route, with no trail or cabins, along the ridge system to the west of the Resurrection Pass Trail. One first climbs to Hope Point, the high spot west of town, and then follows the long ridge system, generally south and winding somewhat, for a couple of days, finally dropping to Swan Lake and joining the Resurrection Pass Trail by Juneau Creek. Except when there is still snow, you will have to carry water during the day to avoid the necessity for long side trips down into creek beds. There are some nice tarns that make a good campsite for the first night about eight or nine miles from the start of the trip at Hope. With a bit of care in looking, water can also be found after another day of hiking under ten miles. Alternatively, a long second day of fifteen miles or so will bring you to Swan Lake. Another day brings you to Cooper Landing, unless he stops for fishing, making the trip of three or four days duration for strong hikers. Weaker parties and those with small children will probably prefer the Resurrection Pass Trail, but this alternative provides spectacular views. It is above timberline from a little above Hope to Swan Lake, and these parallel routes may be attractive for groups with members of varying ability or ambition, since two sub-parties can split, while still following the same general line.

To find the beginning of the high route, continue along the road that goes west from Hope to Porcupine Creek Campground. From the campground, a trail starts up Porcupine Creek on the north side. This trail will get you above timberline, after which it runs out. Climb on up to the local high spot, Hope Point, and then head south along the rounded ridge system, keeping track of your progress with topo and compass, in case the clouds should move in. Again, the large-scale Seward map shows the whole trip. For detail the maps are Seward B8, C8, and D8.

There are many fine trips in McKinley National Park. Except around the immediate area of park headquarters and in some other spots of heavy use, there are no established trails, and this is a real blessing, since concentrated use along trails would cause crowding and damage the delicate tundra. Following the river beds is one good way to find generally easy routes, though crossings may be difficult when water is high.

The Teklanika and Sanctuary Rivers both make good backpacking routes, if the hiker follows them upstream from the bridges on the park road. A nice two-day backpack starts at Sable Pass on the park road, follows Igloo Creek south to its head, and continues south over a pass to the easternmost fork of the East Fork Toklat River. A little way up the river, one can camp at the snout of a glacier, ringed by spectacular peaks, where one may wish to spend some time exploring.

Follow the river downstream for a day's walk back to the road.

For a four- to six-day backpack in the park, one good trip goes to McGonagall Pass, at the edge of the Muldrow Glacier. This is the route followed by McKinley climbers approaching from the north. The standard way begins near Wonder Lake, heading straight for Cache Creek across the McKinley River. This can be a particularly difficult and dangerous crossing when the water is high, and it is not always safe without a rope. Those who would like an easier crossing can begin from Eielson Visitor Center, cross the Thorofare River at the point where it is broken into the greatest number of channels, and then walk across the tongue of the Muldrow Glacier where it is covered with shale and dirt, coming out on the other side of the McKinley River. This route will require an extra day's walking in either direction for strong backpackers. Whichever approach is used, the route then goes up Cache Creek and crosses the pass at its head. From here one can look down on the Muldrow, with a fine view on good weather days. Plan to make your river crossings early in the morning, when the water will be lower.

The whole park is covered on one special sheet, with a scale of 1:250,000, but those intending to backpack in the park should get more detailed sheets for the areas they plan to visit. Of the trips that have been mentioned here, the Teklanika River is on Healy B6 and C6, the Sanctuary on Healy B5 and C5. The trip from Sable Pass up Igloo Creek and down the East Fork Toklat is on Healy B6 and C6. The hike up to McGonagall Pass is on McKinley A2 and B2, and if it is started from Eielson Visitor Center instead of Wonder Lake, B1 will be needed as well. Those wanting an excellent topo map of Mount McKinley itself should obtain the one done by Bradford Washburn and published by the Boston Museum of Science.

7

Canoe and Kayak Travel

Small watercraft have a special advantage for those wishing to explore many regions of the North. They are easily taken in to many takeoff points and can be carried along on a general camping trip for exploration of waters along the way, without the need for cumbersome trailers. Because they can be portaged easily, they provide one of the few suitable ways for exploring areas that are honeycombed with lakes and meandering streams. For the white water enthusiast, Alaska, the Yukon, and northern British Columbia have thousands of miles of challenging rivers, but there are also sections of many northern rivers that are quite slow, and they provide opportunities for incredible wilderness experiences for anyone who has acquired reasonable paddling competence.

Small watercraft will allow the traveler many more opportunities for observation of wildlife than he would ever have on foot. Large mammals are far less likely to be intimidated by a quiet paddler than by a human traveling in any other way. Fishing possibilities are obvious to any dedicated angler.

Perhaps the most attractive feature of travel in the North by canoe and kayak is the ease with which anyone can use them to discover pristine wilderness only a few hundred yards from the road. Foot travel away from the beaten track is often quite difficult in the North, while movement in small watercraft is frequently very easy, particularly in some waterlogged tundra regions.

114

Safety

The usual safety precautions for handling small boats have to be observed, of course, unless one is deliberately courting disaster. These should be learned at home, well before the would-be canoeist or kayaker plans his sojourn on chilly northern streams. Most important are adequate flotation devices, swimming ability, knowledge of the handling characteristics of the crafts, individual skill in handling the kind of water that is to be navigated, and avoidance of overloading. Well-developed technique in the use of a compass and map is also vital, particularly in river deltas and complexes of tundra lakes.

Northern waters are always very cold, and this must be taken into account when considering safety. It makes no difference how good a swimmer one is after a few minutes in the water of a glacial stream without protection for the body. Swimming any distance to shore or holding onto a flotation device for long periods is impossible for anyone wearing normal clothing. Canoeists should consider the possibility and likelihood of a capsize. Dry clothing in a watertight bag attached to the canoe might be a lifesaver after a tip in the middle of a big lake. Life jackets are often indicated, particularly if any white water is to be run. Wet suits are often a necessity for kayakers and are sometimes a good idea for canoeists as well. A full wet suit $\frac{3}{16}''$ thick is mandatory for any serious white water paddling in the North. Cold water conditions should be taken into account before running any rapids, with prudence often indicating portaging or lining the boat around white water.

Other Watercraft

Many other kinds of boats, besides canoes and kayaks, are of course suitable for trips in northern waters. One can use normal small boats of any kind on the big lakes that are accessible by road. Rubber rafts may be chosen for fishing or downriver trips. Shallow-draft boats of all kinds are used on the big, slow rivers like the Yukon. Kayaks and canoes are simply the most versatile and portable craft for getting to, and traveling on, wilderness waterways.

Getting There and Back

There are many circuit trips of moderate distance that can be made in the North from put-in points along the road systems, and these need no special attention. One can spend a few hours or a few weeks exploring a lake that is accessible from the highway, just as one does nearer home. One of the great attractions of the North, however, is the vast wilderness region far from the reach of the automobile. With five minutes at the map collection, the wilderness lover can plan enough trips along the wild waterways of the North to last several lifetimes. Usually, one of the major problems to be solved is that of getting you and your boat to the beginning of the trip and back from the end.

It would be quite possible to gain access to many areas of the deep wilderness by using paddle and portage alone, but the time factor would enter here. Several years might be required for the entire journey, as it was for many of the first Europeans to enter some of the vast country. Most of us do not have so much time to spend and thus have to rely on modern means of transportation to get us there and back.

There are tens of thousands of miles of peaceful rivers and lakes stretching across country of incomparable beauty in Alaska and northern Canada. Canoes and kayaks are ideal for exploring them.

The least expensive trips of this kind, and the simplest to plan, are those that reach the waterways by car, putting in where the road comes close to a river or lake and making a rendezvous at some other point, usually downriver. One popular trip of two or three weeks follows the Yukon River from Whitehorse in the Yukon Territory to Circle in Alaska. Both are accessible by road, so with two cars and a week or so of shuttle driving, it is simple enough to plan this trip. Shorter versions of the same journey on the Yukon can make use of the access points between Dawson City and Eagle. Paddlers in search of more challenging and less frequented trips can easily devise routes from a roadhead in one watershed to one in another, portaging across intervening dry ground. There are various other transportation possibilities; a fishing boat may be hired to take you along the coast from the mouth of a river to a larger town or into a protected inlet, for example. Air travel is the most likely way to get to or from points that cannot be reached by car, however. Despite its small population, the North has an extensive network of commercial pilots who will hire out to take you into the backcountry and pick you up a month later. Many are equipped with pontoons, so that they can easily land at a suitable lake, weather permitting.

The biggest problem, if you plan to travel partway by air, is carrying your canoe or kayak. The folding kayaks are particularly suitable for this kind of trip, because they can be easily packed into the main cargo area of even the smallest planes. Rigid canoes and kayaks are too large to be fit into small bush planes, and if they are strapped on the bottom of the fuselage, the flying characteristics of the aircraft are changed. Some bush pilots will be able to take your canoe in, and some will not. Prior correspondence is essential for those planning to have a rigid canoe or kayak flown into the bush.

Clearly, with any long trip, careful planning of food and equipment is essential. Reliable gear, repair kits, extra paddles, and the like must be brought. If you plan to rendezvous with a plane, be sure to nail everything down in advance. Allow plenty of time to get to the meeting place. Be sure that you and the pilot can find it, arrange for signals, and agree on what is to be done if you don't get there or if there is a stretch of bad flying weather.

Picking a Trip

Most people, at least on their first trip north, will not choose a month-long trip involving flying in and out. A two-week paddle around one or two lakes or river systems is more likely. Some special considerations should be borne in mind even for such modest expeditions.

Big lakes, particularly those as cold as the great lakes of Alaska and the Yukon area, must be treated with considerable respect. Heavy winds can raise large waves, and these can present real navigational difficulties even for an expert paddler. For a relative novice, a squall on a big lake can be deadly. It is important to remain aware of your limits. Don't get too far from shore, particularly when there are signs of a storm or heavy wind. For those of limited experience, it is much safer to stay fairly close to shore and to put in if the wind comes up. Similarly, be wary when you must pass long sections of shoreline without good beaches. A three-mile-long band of cliffs with an onshore wind presents serious problems. Similar cautions apply with even more force to difficult stretches of river running. Novices should stick to the easiest of wilderness rivers or portage around difficulties.

Some investigation needs to be made if you are planning a trip in an early or late season. For instance, the ice does not usually go out on Kluane Lake until June, making an early May canoe trip there impractical.

Portages and route-finding difficulties will vary a good deal with the area, so those who are relatively inexperienced should get as much information as possible before deciding whether a trip is within their capacities. Muskeg areas with networks of fallen black spruce can be particularly hard to portage, and rain forests are often virtually impossible to cross without a trail. Boggy regions also present severe mosquito problems except in the late fall. Big rivers and lakes are usually breezier and thus much freer of bugs. Some deltas and broad, flat areas along the larger rivers present serious navigational difficulties, as do large networks of small lakes. Those with only minimal experience in wilderness route finding are well advised to take their first trips in country where the way is easy to find.

Some of the most obvious trips, suitable for beginners or

experts and easy to get to, begin with the great lakes that are accessible by the road system extending through the North. There is a major chain of huge lakes in the country north of the Prince Rupert Highway: Babine Lake, Takla, Stuart, and a host of smaller lakes that form a great wilderness network. This is a lovely region and is of easy access. The body of water now building up behind the W.A.C. Bennett Dam, Williston Lake, should be avoided, however. The timber from the flooded area will form a navigation hazard there for many years.

Muncho Lake Provincial Park in British Columbia along the Alaska Highway presents the opportunity for some attractive short trips. Farther north along the Alcan is the huge network of large lakes that form the headwaters of the Yukon River: Teslin, Atlin, Little Atlin, Taku Arm, Laberge, and hundreds of others cover vast areas of wilderness that could occupy the visitor for as long as he chooses to stay. This system is accessible from several points along the highway.

There are many lakes and rivers accessible from the new western road that meets the Alcan at Watson Lake. Many of the lakes and streams along this road are still virtually unexplored. Others have a history running back to gold rush days, like the Stikine River, which formed a link in one of the many difficult routes to the Klondike. Kitsumkalum Lake and Kitwanga Lake are found on the two approaches to the Stewart Road. (See chapter 1 for more details on their location.) Farther north, the road provides access to the Nass River, which has interesting possibilities for experienced river travelers. Other rivers along this route are also fine waterways for those who can plan for and deal with wilderness white water and with the fjords into which they empty, but these rugged rivers should be avoided by the unseasoned. Meziadin Lake, which now has a provincial campground on its shore, is

For those who enjoy the challenge of white water, the North is the last great refuge from the dam-builders, and there are literally hundreds of rivers that have never been run.

a lovely place for family outings and is large enough so that the access by road is quickly forgotten once one has paddled around the corner; the rest of the lake is wilderness. Other large lakes on this road include Kinaskan, Eddontenajon, and Dease.

Two of the greatest wilderness river systems in the world can be approached from the Alaska Highway. The Yukon River has already been mentioned. The Mackenzie River, which finally ends in the Arctic Ocean, is also accessible from the Alcan. As with the Yukon, one can put in at one point of the river system and shuttle cars to another point hundreds of miles away. The Liard River is reached from several points on the highway in northern British Columbia, and it empties into the Mackenzie. Some distance farther, the Mackenzie itself can be approached by car at Canol in the Northwest Territories; the Canol Road leaves the Alcan at Johnson's Crossing (mile 836). As with the Yukon, a river trip to the mouth of the Mackenzie will require arrangements to come out by air, since Canol is the last place that is accessible by road. The Mackenzie can also be reached by road farther east at Great Slave Lake. Those considering this trip are cautioned that the Liard has some dangerous rapids that require portaging or considerable white water experience. This river should be avoided by all but the most seasoned wilderness travelers.

Another good trip for boaters with experience in traveling wilderness rivers with some white water is the Macmillan River from the crossing of the South Macmillan on the Canol Road to the Dawson Road.

In Alaska itself there are so many possibilities that only a few can be mentioned. The Yukon has already been discussed. A shorter trip on a river accessible by auto is the lower Susitna River, which can be reached from many points along the Anchorage-Fairbanks highway. Tributary rivers and nearby lakes provide opportunities for wilderness travel without the need for hiring an airplane.

There are two beautiful canoe routes on the Kenai Peninsula starting from the Swan Lake Road near Sterling. Both the Swan Lake Canoe Route and the Swanson River Canoe Route are suitable for novices. Though experts could finish either in a couple of days, a leisurely family vacation might be spent with a week or ten days allocated to one of these routes. Information on these and some other suggested waterways can be found in a pamphlet, *Alaska Canoe Trails*, obtainable from the Bureau of Land Management at the address listed in chapter 11.

Those searching for trips into very remote regions, far from the nearest road might consider a trip down the Colville

This is the put-in for an easy but very long river trip. The sign says most of it; in that 1,980 miles, there are fewer than ten points accessible by road.

River, north of the Brooks Range in the arctic tundra, or the more rugged Noatak, which drains to the west. There is stark and beautiful country around Clark Lake, north of the Alaska Peninsula, and there are a host of fine, large lakes along the Alaska Peninsula. The Charley River, a tributary of the Yukon, is one of the clearest Alaskan rivers. A plane has to be taken in, if one is not ready for difficult upriver work, but one can exit on the Yukon at Circle.

Those searching for white water thrills can find good trips of intermediate difficulty on the Kenai River below Skilak Lake, on the Gulkana River from Paxon Lake to Gulkana, and on Birch Creek between its two crossings of the Steese Highway. For the adventurous, there are countless rapids awaiting the finding on the many wilderness rivers of Alaska, the Yukon, and northern British Columbia.

Equipment and Provisioning

All equipment for water trips should be packed in watertight containers that are well secured to your boat. Plenty of warm clothes and adequate shelter for wet weather are essential. Lightweight synthetic-filled bags have some advantage over down in prolonged wet weather and around water. They dry quickly and retain some loft even when wet. Great care must be taken to keep down gear dry if it is used. In damp weather, stuff your down bag or jacket into a watertight storage sack as soon as you get out of it, before it cools and moisture condenses in the insulation. By stuffing the down gear, you squeeze the moist air out before condensation occurs.

Consider carrying a stove, particularly if you are traveling one of the more heavily used routes or if you are going to tundra regions. If you build fires, you will need to take a light saw and perhaps an ax. In wet climates, the ax will be necessary to split out dry wood. Use only dead wood, preferably dead wood that is already down. Be extremely careful with fire. Build only on bare mineral soil; sandbars are excellent. If you build on a rock, cover it with sand or solid soil first to avoid new fire scars. If there is a fireplace built already, use it; the wilderness experience is as fragile as the wilderness itself—the enjoyment of others who come after you will be diminished by the debris you abandon. Try to leave the country as pristine as you found it, as though you had never been there.

8

Mountain Travel and Ski Touring

The subject of this chapter is far too specialized to permit very detailed discussion. A whole book could easily be written on the subject of Alaskan mountaineering alone, even for a specialized audience of accomplished climbers. The main purpose of this short section is to give climbers and ski tourers an idea of the special problems that they should expect when planning a trip north. There is no space here for a primer on mountaineering or snow travel, and novices are cautioned that Alaska is an unforgiving place to learn basic skills in these demanding sports.

Conditions in the high mountains and the winters of the North are characterized by much harsher weather than that found in temperate zones. As has been mentioned in earlier chapters, the climatic extremes will vary a great deal with exact location, particularly with distance from the sea and the positions of other geographic features, which may trap cold air, deflect the movements of storms or remove most of their moisture, or otherwise affect the climate of the whole area. In general, sections near the ocean will have more moderate temperatures, but snow is likely to be deeper and wetter than in inland regions. As one moves farther north or farther inland, low temperatures will drop, and the snow will come less frequently, be drier, and last longer into the spring.

The Mountains

Mountaineers are familiar with the fact that a small increase in altitude has effects on climate similar to traveling some distance north. The visitor familiar with peaks south of Canada may be confused at first by the way this factor operates in the mountains of Alaska and the Yukon. Here the snowline may go to sea level, and the effects of recent glaciation and the permanent snow lying on the peaks may easily convince the traveler that he is viewing a 14,000-foot mountain, when he is really seeing a 5,000-foot one. This strangeness is likely to throw off the mountain walker's perception of distance as well as his evaluation of the peaks. The illusion has some validity, however, since small mountains in the North are often more serious undertakings than much larger ones in more southerly climes. An assault on an Alaskan 14,000-foot peak will require mounting an expedition.

For the mountaineer, geographical position is especially important. A range of mountains will take the brunt of any storms that pass over it, so that a few miles difference in the position of the peak from the coast, or the interposition of another range of mountains along the storm path will make fantastic differences in weather conditions on the mountain. The mountains all along the Alaskan and British Columbian coasts have extremely severe weather and very large glaciers. Where the glaciers leading to a coastal peak do not drop directly into the sea, the rain forests and the effects of recent glacial activity present staggering approach problems. The Alaska Range is not close to the coast and is not surrounded by rain forests, but since it is the first barrier encountered by storms sweeping in from the Aleutians, it also receives very severe weather. Approach problems through boggy flats and over rushing torrents can be quite formidable as well.

On the other hand, approaches in many other areas are quite reasonable for wilderness mountains. The Brooks Range, for example, with its magnificent crags, sculpted by ancient glaciers, is surrounded by tundra that makes for good backpacking when it is not too wet. Each mountain region in the North has its own characteristics, and problems may vary from blowdown, to river crossings, to holes left by receding glaciers and partly covered by vegetation.

The two main mountain systems of the western United States, the Rocky Mountains and the Coast Ranges, continue up through Canada and bend westward into Alaska. As in the contiguous United States, these great mountain chains have many complex subsidiary ranges. Many hidden outcroppings in Alaska and the Yukon remain essentially unexplored, though they would be major climbing areas, were they not so remote.

The Coast Range of British Columbia extends up from the North Cascades of Washington, forming an extension of the great Pacific cordillera, which includes the Sierra Nevada in California. The true coastal mountains of the North, corresponding to the California Coast Range and the Olympics in Washington, are mostly on islands along the coast, clear into the Panhandle region of Alaska. The Coast Range, and its northern extensions into the Yukon and Alaska, are extremely rugged and very heavily glaciated. Around the Yukon-Alaska border, the Fairweather Range and the Saint Elias Range connect with the Coast Ranges. The Saint Elias mountains are particularly high and spectacular, including 19,850-foot Mount Logan, probably the largest mountain massif in the world. Parts of this beautiful range can be seen from the Alaska Highway, the Marine Route, and the connecting road to Haines Junction. Farther north this Pacific mountain system splits, with the northern crest forming the Alaska Range, the huge set of peaks south of Fairbanks and the Yukon River system. The Alaska Range is dominated by Mount McKinley, the highest peak in North America (20,320 ft.). Several highways lead through this range at low passes and they afford superb views when the peaks are clear. Farther south, the Chugach, Wrangell, and Kenai Mountains are generally lower, though quite spectacular, and sections of these ranges provide opportunities for non-expeditionary mountaineering and mountain travel. The coastal system then continues through spectacular wilderness to the Alaska Peninsula, along it, and out to the Aleutian Islands. There is a great deal of volcanic activity in these southwestern extensions of the uplift. Katmai National Monument, the scene of a tremendous eruption in 1912, is on the Peninsula, as are many other fascinating features, such as the Aniakchak Crater.

The Rocky Mountain system has extensions through much of British Columbia, including both the main bulwark of the Canadian Rockies, which is very remote in the northern part of the province, and many subsidiary chains to the west of the crest, known collectively as the Interior Ranges of British Columbia. The northern extensions of the Interior Ranges, the Omineca and Cassiar Mountains, while not extremely high, are very beautiful and little known. In the Yukon, the Rocky Mountain cordillera extends in a great curve of mountains known collectively as the Mackenzie Mountains. Two branches of the Rockies extend into Alaska: the small ranges between the Tanana and the Yukon, north of Fairbanks, are the White Mountains; and the great chain of mountains known as the Brooks Range extends across Alaska, its north slope and the tundra below dropping to the Arctic Ocean.

Mountain Travel

It should be emphasized that virtually all mountain travel in the North is true wilderness travel. There are very few trails in existence, and the backpacker must be completely self-reliant. All supplies and equipment must be well-suited to the trip, and the group should be very experienced before undertaking a mountain trip. A good deal of advance research will be required for realistic planning. Food, fuel, medical supplies, and protection against rain, insects, and cold need special attention.

Except in the lowest and most arid mountains, experience and equipment for steep snow will be necessary. Ice axes and crampons, together with experience in their proper use, will often be essential even for crossing low passes. If any glacier travel is planned, the party will need ropes and practical experience in crevasse rescue techniques. When there is still soft snow, skis or snowshoes will be needed. When traveling on or near any steep snow slopes, possible avalanche hazards need to be carefully weighed. For any extensive travel on large glaciers, icefields, and permanent snowfields, the party will have to give careful consideration to the problems that might be caused by storm or fog. It is often necessary to mark such routes with wands (willow sticks), to do extensive compass work, or both.

Areas which still have large glaciers, as do the coastal regions, sometimes present special problems. Besides the heavy vegetation that may be present, unstable ground is sometimes found near the tongues of glaciers that have recently receded. Vegetation may begin to grow in debris left on top of a moraine, even before the ice below has melted, so that later a cavity may form beneath the ground. This hazard is present, for example, in some regions near Juneau.

Low peaks in McKinley National Park.

These cautions are not meant to discourage the backcountry wanderer, merely to point out that trips into rugged wilderness mountains should not be undertaken lightly and without preparation. For the neophyte, it is best to begin by encountering such country first via existing trails or on journeys starting from a road and lasting only a few days, rather than by plunging immediately into an area that requires considerable experience and a special taste for difficulty.

Mountaineering

The variety of objectives available to the mountaineer in the North is nearly as wide as the range of climbing itself.

There are mountains for conventional peak-baggers, great rock walls for modern technical climbers, and huge, snow-covered giants to attract the expeditionary mountaineer. Hence, it is difficult to generalize in a meaningful way about the climbing. Approach problems are usually difficult, particularly for those with limited time. Most climbers hire a plane, equipped for landing on snow or water, depending on the objective, to fly them as close to their mountains as possible. There are many pilots in Alaska who are experienced in dropping mountaineers on glaciers in the wildest ranges. There is a great deal of reward in getting to one's goal by foot or boat, however, when this can be managed. Anyone planning such serious expeditionary work is foolish if he does not accumulate as much information as possible first. There is a multitude of pitfalls awaiting the climber new to the big ranges, from the problems of dividing loads properly to those of making prior arrangements with the pilot concerning pickups, emergencies, and the like.

In any kind of mountaineering, it is important to remember the differences in the climate of the North. Avalanche cycles are likely to be quite different than those a climber is used to. In the big ranges, snowslides can be of immense scale, sweeping across a valley and up the other side. Cold temperatures may cause dangerous avalanche conditions to persist for long periods, even in summer. Severe weather must be expected on any northern peak at any time of the year.

There are some exceptions, but most northern mountains have long periods of bad weather, and this must be taken into account in planning schedules, equipment, and attitudes. In some sections of the coast, mountains may receive nearly two hundred inches of rain in a year, so that precipitation is almost continuous, and even at high altitudes the snow may be wet. The best chance for reasonable weather is in the mountains far to the north and in the interior, but even there, wet ground conditions are the rule at lower elevations, because permafrost a few inches below the surface traps moisture above. Mountaineers should pay particular attention to footwear, clothing, tents, sleeping bags, and rain gear, with consideration for the problems of wet insulation on a mountain.

For the mountaineer looking for an introductory trip in the mountains of the North, without the formidable extra difficulties posed by the big peaks and the remote wilderness, there are many fine mountains close to the road between Haines Junction and Haines, near Kluane Lake in the Yukon, and in the Kenai and Chugach Ranges in Alaska. Some of these peaks are easy climbs within a day's reach from the road or trail, while some can be quite challenging. All are at relatively low altitudes and present climbing problems similar to those of Washington, Wyoming, or Colorado. Some of the low mountains in McKinley National Park also make good introductory Alaskan climbs.

Ski Touring

Though few visitors go to Alaska, the Yukon, and northern British Columbia during the snowy months, the possibilities for the enthusiastic ski tourer are limitless. Whether he is interested in day trips on perfect cold powder snow or in extended wilderness trips, opportunities for the skier abound.

Conditions are generally cold everywhere, and they are extremely severe in the interior. Anyone planning a ski trip, however short, in the region needs a thorough knowledge of winter survival techniques. Clothing for very cold weather must be worn or carried. Face masks are essential. Lightweight boots are inadequate. Double boots or insulated overboots are mandatory, since snow temperatures can be very cold even if the air is relatively warm. Remember that in the winter months the sun will probably never rise above the ridge, even in southeastern Alaska.

Tourers skiing near any of the population centers will generally have to put up with snowmobile traffic, particularly on weekends. From the Alaska Highway, there are good tours from many of the big lakes in the Yukon. Near Anchorage, there is a nice marked ski trail that is barred to snowmobiles on the east side of the Seward Highway at mile 69. McKinley National Park offers excellent possibilities for trips of almost any length.

The season for skiing varies in the North as elsewhere, depending on altitude, latitude, and local climate. Snow is usually good even at lower elevations into April in southern Alaska; somewhat later as one goes higher, farther north, or farther inland.

9

Bush Pilots, Guides, and Camps

True wilderness regions are, by definition, not readily accessible by road. Definitions will vary, but much of the far North is wilderness by the strictest definition, remote, devoid of roads or trails, showing few signs or none of contact with people. There are mountains that have been neither named nor climbed, lakes that no one has stood by within living memory. There are also vast areas that are traveled by people, but only rarely, dense and trackless forests, lakes teeming with fish, great and lonely spaces.

Many such places have never been explored by people, others have been visited only by Indians or Eskimos. The exploration that did occur was made with a good deal of hardship and sacrifice. A party could spend years getting into some of these regions. Transportation by foot and canoe over such distances is slow indeed, and for food, the explorer had to live off the land, killing animals as he went to keep himself alive.

The modern wilderness camper or traveler is fortunate in being able to visit the most remote corners of the North without having to make long treks in or leaving a trail of litter and dead animals behind. He can land on a lake or glacier and minutes later be completely alone, as the sound of the departing plane fades away. He can be picked up weeks later and leave the country as he found it, with hardly a trace of his passing. One of the great virtues of planes for transportation in the wild parts of the continent is that they allow people to use the wilderness with minimum impact.

Such use of small planes is not necessarily too expensive, even for visitors of modest means. The cost is likely to be between $50 and $100 per hour for plane and pilot, depending on the type of plane and the kind of flying involved. Though you must pay for round trip on both your flight in and the one out, a small plane will travel fast enough so that an hour takes you a long way. When the cost is divided among several people, it is often quite reasonable. The number of people and the amount of equipment that can be carried depend on the plane and the trip, but advance correspondence with your pilot will give you a good idea of your costs.

It may be possible to reduce the expense of being flown in still farther if you can fly with a bush pilot who covers a regular route, delivering mail and supplies to isolated settlements. In such a case, dropping you at a lake along the way may involve only a slight detour, and charges may be reduced accordingly.

Regularly scheduled flights stop at many small communities in Alaska, and it is often possible to plan wilderness trips to begin or end at such towns to reduce the cost of a trip. Be sure to have a clear understanding before you leave as to when planes arrive, how regular they are, whether they have to be signaled to stop, and so on.

Use of planes to fly in is not at all limited to mountaineers and fanatic backpackers. A fine family outing can be planned using a plane to fly to a remote lake, where a tent can be set up and everyone can enjoy a relaxed vacation fishing, swimming, hiking, or just lying around. Similarly one can fly to one of the isolated Forest Service cabins, which rent for $5 per day and often include use of a boat. The one thing common to all trips where the party is flown in is that members are virtually guaranteed as much solitude as they want.

Planning a Trip Using a Bush Pilot

The first step in planning a trip will depend somewhat on your purposes. If you have a specific objective in mind—a particular lake, a mountain, a backpack trip from one point to another—then the first step is to find a pilot who will be able to get you there and back most economically. If you are thinking more generally, then you may wish first to decide on one area, with climate, scenery, and rainfall in mind, and then correspond with a pilot who flies in that region, asking him for recommendations. (Addresses to write for lists of licensed bush pilots are given in chapter 11.) Many bush pilots know the country they fly extremely well, and they can probably give you as good advice as you will find anywhere on the spot you should pick.

Working out a specific trip involves several steps. Suppose that you decide on a backpacking trip from one lake to another in a remote area of Alaska. You can get a list of bush pilots from the division of tourism, and from this list you can find the name of a pilot who operates a float plane as close to your starting point and your destination as possible. Correspond with the pilot, asking whether he is available at the time you want to go and return, what his rates are, how many trips would be required to take your party and gear (you'll have to give him an idea of the weight involved and any special large items such as canoes), and what his estimate of total flying time would be. As a rough idea, round trip to a lake fifty miles away from his base would probably involve about one and a half hours, including unloading time.

For the fisherman or the canoeist, the bush pilot provides the means of getting to lakes like this, without another person for miles around.

Another one and a half hours would be required to pick you up, making a total of three hours. You'll then have a pretty good idea of how much the trip would cost, and you can go on with your plans, making definite arrangements with the pilot, and so forth.

If there are several pilots near your proposed destination, it is a good idea to write to all of them. This is true not only because some rates may be lower, but because many bush pilots have regular arrangements which may make them unavailable at some times of the year. From August on through fall, a large number are engaged to fly hunting parties. You may also be able to get by much more cheaply with a particular pilot because of the type of plane he uses. If you had a party of four, you might find that one pilot with a small plane would have to take two or three trips to get you all in with your equipment, while another could take you all in one flight because he had a larger plane. In this case the larger plane will probably be cheaper, even though the rate per hour is higher.

If you plan to be flown both in and out, be sure that the arrangement between you and your pilot is completely clear on both sides before you start. You must allow for the possibility of bad flying weather. Have plenty of food, and be sure that you know when the pilot will come back if visibility is bad on his first attempt. He may have another obligation the following day, and you will want to know when to expect him if he can't get to you at the agreed time. Make sure that you agree on the financial arrangements if he flies in and cannot land because of ground fog; you will probably have to pay for his flying time even if he cannot land.

There are few complications in all this if the pilot is to pick you up at the same spot, but if you are on a long cross-country trip, it is vital to be sure you understand one another and have planned for contingencies. Be sure to allow yourself enough time to reach your destination; if you are late you will still have to pay the pilot for flying in to get you. Have a precise understanding of what the pilot is to do if you are not there. You may want him to come back a specified number of days later and then begin a search if you have still not arrived. Be sure all such details are arranged and that the pilot knows you are willing to pay for whatever service you want. Make sure that you both have a precise understanding of where you are to be picked up and how you will be spotted. Lakes can begin to look very similar in some country, and in a forested region it can be virtually impossible to see people on the ground from an airplane. Even on tundra, something like a bright orange tent will make the party much more visible. Careful consultation of maps with the pilot before you leave is essential. Remember that maps in these regions are imperfect.

Mountaineers who wish to land on glaciers can find pilots with specially equipped planes, which have hydraulically operated skis that are dropped below the wheels for landing on snow. Glacier landings are a very tricky business; few pilots venture into this sort of thing, and it is usually best to get in touch with other climbers who have been to the particular range in which you are interested to get recommendations. In the most popular area, the Alaska Range south of McKinley National Park, Talkeetna flyers Don Sheldon and Cliff Hudson both have admirable and well-deserved reputations.

Mountaineers and those planning very long backpacks in remote regions may want to have air drops of food along the route. This requires even more careful logistical planning with the pilot, who somehow has to find you along the way. Containers have to be strong, with everything packed extremely well. Fuel for stoves is hard to drop successfully at all, though jerry cans sometimes survive the fall. For backpackers, when lakes are available along the route, it usually makes more sense to plant a cache on the flight in, taking proper precautions to protect it from animals.

Guides

There are many guides in the North, particularly for those who are interested in hunting and fishing. Hunting guides must be licensed and lists of guides in Alaska or in one of the Canadian political subdivisions can be obtained from the appropriate agencies, which are listed in chapter 11.

Many guides are also qualified bush pilots and they

frequently maintain camps for their clients. Hunting is expensive for nonresidents, and the services of guides are likely to come high also. Those wishing to engage the services of guides for other purposes, however, may be able to get a reasonable rate early in the year, before hunting season begins. Depending on the species and area, hunting season normally starts sometime in August or September, so that if you plan a trip earlier, you may be able to obtain reduced rates. Most guides are booked well in advance, so it is important to begin correspondence long before you plan your trip.

Guide services specializing in backpacking trips, canoeing, kayaking, ski touring, and mountaineering are becoming more common, though there are still only a few. Some are listed in chapter 11.

Camps

Most camps that are associated with guide services are actually resorts. One that deserves special mention, however, is Camp Denali, located at the heart of McKinley National Park (though technically outside the park boundary), and run by people with a real appreciation for the park. Camp Denali has both cabins and tents, and visitors can either cook for themselves or purchase prepared meals. The proprietors are always pleased to give advice on approaching the surrounding wilderness, whether on short hikes or long backpacking trips. They also supply equipment and guides. You can write them at Box D, College, Alaska 99701.

10

Fishing

Many of the waters in the North are a paradise for the fisherman, simply because the ratio of fish to anglers is very high. This is particularly true when one gets away from those streams close to population centers. It is especially fine country for the novice, because the fish are less "educated" than the wily residents of heavily fished waters close to home.

It would be a hopeless and unproductive task to try to catalogue the good fishing in the North. One of the main attractions of Alaska and northwestern Canada for the fisherman is that no one knows even a fraction of the good fishing spots.

The keys accompanying many of the maps in this book include some recommended fishing spots that are easily accessible. The best fishing of all, however, will be found in those places that are rarely visited, requiring a plane ride, a boat trip, or a long walk in. The new sections of the Coast Range Highway are particularly recommended for fresh water fishing, but it is not hard to find a private fishing spot almost anywhere in the North.

In general, any of the reasonably clear lakes and rivers in the North will have good fishing. There are many streams fed by glaciers which are an opaque white, gray, or green from "glacial milk," consisting of fine particles ground from surrounding rocks by the moving ice of the glaciers and washed along by the water melted from the ice. Such waters generally provide poor fishing until they have run far enough

141

to drop most of their mineral burden. Similarly, large rivers that are very silty usually are not good for fishing, but tributary streams feeding into them may be excellent. Tarns in alpine and tundra regions vary a good deal in fishing quality, depending on whether they freeze solid in the winter, whether they dry out in some years, and whether fish have ever managed to get to them.

Licenses and Regulations

It is, of course, illegal to fish without a license in most cases. Since closed areas and seasons vary from year to year, anglers should be sure to obtain a copy of current rules when they purchase licenses. In British Columbia, Canadians eighteen or over pay $3 for a season license, while those under eighteen are not required to have permits. Non-Canadians pay $15 for a season license, $6 for a short-term permit good for three consecutive days, and $1 for a season permit for those under eighteen. An additional license is required to fish for steelheads for anglers over eighteen: $2 for Canadians and $10 for others. In the Yukon, those over sixteen must have licenses, which cost $3 a year for those residing in Canada, $10 for nonresidents, or $3.50 for a five-day license for non-Canadians. In Alaska licenses are required of those over sixteen, and for nonresidents they cost $20 a season or $10 for a ten-day permit.

Tackle

Equipment will vary a good deal depending on your own attitudes and on the type of fish you are trying to take. As elsewhere, both fly and spinning gear have their particular uses. Light equipment will normally be used for cutthroat, Kokanee, grayling, and other smaller fish. Heavier fly or spinning tackle is usually used for lake trout and similar larger fish, while fairly heavy tackle will be chosen by most anglers seeking king salmon, silver salmon, or steelheads. Salt water fishing requires the usual salt water gear. Some additional comments on equipment are made in discussing particular fish.

The Fish

Arctic char are fine game fish of the far North, frequenting the mouths of rivers and streams feeding down to the sea all along the arctic coast. Arctic char replace Dolly Varden trout as one moves farther north. (Dolly Varden are found at the mouths of streams in southeastern Alaska.) The two may be found together in many rivers from the Kenai Peninsula north, with arctic char becoming more dominant and Dolly Varden disappearing on the north slope of the Brooks Range. Char may also be found inland, though they tend to predominate closer to river mouths. Spinning is usually quite effective.

Arctic grayling are also widely distributed northern fish of cold streams and lakes. They are found in large numbers throughout most of the North, particularly in interior regions. Many of the large lakes along the highway systems have excellent grayling fishing. Light fly tackle is effective and provides good fishing.

Burbot is a large fish of the interior lakes and is usually taken by fishing from a boat with bait.

Cutthroat trout is the fine small game trout of the coastal streams of British Columbia and southeastern Alaska. Some stay in fresh water all the time, while others move back and

These gulls have found that the fishing is good in this lake, and so have the few fishermen who have tried their luck here.

forth between the rivers and salt water. Cutthroat can be taken with flies, spinning gear, or bait, using light- or medium-weight tackle.

Dolly Varden is a very widespread and popular trout which inhabits the coastal rivers from British Columbia to the Seward Peninsula, gradually being replaced by arctic char at the northern extent of its range. Dollies may spend all their time in fresh water, and are sometimes found in lakes and streams far inland, but coastal rivers and creeks are prime habitat, and the best Dolly Varden fishing is near the mouths of streams emptying into salt water. Tackle and fishing methods are similar to those used for cutthroat and other small to medium trout.

Kokanee are actually small fresh water salmon found in many lakes in British Columbia and a few along the

Panhandle and the Kenai Peninsula in Alaska. They are delicious eating fish and are most frequently taken with light spinning gear.

Lake trout is the largest of trout, and the big, cold lakes of the North are his preferred habitat. In the North, lake trout can be found at a moderate distance from the surface for much longer periods than in warmer lakes to the south, though spring and fall still provide the best fishing. Aside from trolling, the most likely choice of equipment will be a bait casting rod and reel with a good-sized spoon. Let the spoon go all the way to the bottom and then retrieve it quickly.

Northern pike is a fine game fish found in the cold interior lakes and streams of Alaska and the Yukon. It can be taken with a bait casting rod, but a medium-weight spinning rod makes things more interesting. Medium and large spoons or spinners are the best lures.

Rainbow trout are familiar to most fishermen and are found here and there throughout the area except in the northern sections of Alaska and the Yukon. Northern British Columbia provides excellent rainbow fishing in most of the large lakes and coastal streams. Tackle is typical fly or spinning tackle for trout, with flies, spinners, spoons, and salmon eggs all working well in suitable conditions.

Salmon is probably the most sought-after game fish in Alaska and British Columbia and is also the most abused by illegal fishing methods, since salmon has very regular migrations and a large relative size when going up spawning streams. Five species of salmon are found in the area. In size, they range upward from the *pink salmon*, the size of a big rainbow trout, through the *red salmon* and the *chum salmon*, to the real prizes, the *silver salmon* and the great *king salmon*. The best season for salmon varies a good deal with the location. Early spring and late fall tend to be best in the coastal streams of the Panhandle and the British Columbian coast, while the season comes later in spring as one moves farther north. The smaller species are generally later than the kings. Salmon are migratory species, and their annual movements are quite predictable, so it is best to consult knowledgeable local people about times to fish particular streams. Regulations for salmon fishing are quite strict, so consult detailed regulations before you go fishing. Snagging of king salmon (an illegal fishing technique) has greatly reduced the number of fish in many popular areas. Salmon taste best, fight hardest, and are most likely to take a lure as they come in from the sea, so fishing is best far downstream from spawning grounds, though a visit to spawning streams is very interesting. (Do watch out for bears.) Spoons and bait, particularly herring, work well on salmon, except for red salmon, which are best taken with flies. Tackle weight will depend on the species. Light and medium tackle is adequate for all but silver and king, for which steelhead or heavier equipment will be required.

Steelhead trout are sea-going rainbows that are famous game fish. They spend a couple of years in fresh water, migrate out to sea, and then return to their home rivers to spawn, though they do not necessarily die there like salmon. Steelhead are found in coastal rivers as far north as Kodiak Island and are generally caught in early spring or late fall. Salmon eggs and artificial lures are both effective.

Whitefish are trout-sized fish of the lakes and streams of the interior and mountains. They can be caught with normal trout tackle and methods.

Other fish are present besides those mentioned here, particularly in salt water. Good salt water fishing can be had all through the islands of British Columbia and Alaska, and boats which can be hired are easy to find. Halibut running to a couple of hundred pounds can be taken. Shellfish can be

Some lake fishermen are enthusiastic enough to tow their boats over hundreds of miles of gravel roads to get to lakes like this one in northern British Columbia. At many Forest Service cabins in Alaska, the boat is included.

found at many places along the coast, including crabs, clams, and razor clams. Smelt can also be dipped along the coast at many places.

Where and When to Go

If I were going to the North specifically for fishing, I would probably visit some of the coastal streams and lakes of northern British Columbia or the Alaskan Panhandle in May, a time when there are many migratory runs. You can take the ferries to one of the coastal towns and then hire a float plane for a short jaunt to an isolated lake that can be used as a base of operations. Those wanting all the comforts of home, and often a boat as well, can use one of the Forest Service cabins in the Tongass National Forest for $5 per day for the whole party.

There is an infinite variety of other trips that would also provide superb fishing, for example, taking a boat up to some of the big interior lakes or fishing the river and lakes along the new Coast Range Highway. Wherever you go in the North, you're likely to have good fishing.

11

Where to Get More Information

Government sources will supply a wealth of information about Alaska, the Yukon, and British Columbia, so the prospective traveler should not have too much difficulty finding out what he needs to know. Tourism is a major industry in the North, and travel routes are few, so planning conventional trips is fairly easy. Those going off the beaten track will have to do a bit more research, since much of the vast northern backcountry is visited rarely, if at all. Only a few of the possible sources of information are mentioned here, but they will be adequate for most campers and should lead the adventurous to other possibilities.

General Information

Alaska: Alaska Travel Division, Pouch E, Juneau, Alaska 99801.

British Columbia: Department of Travel Industry, Government of British Columbia, Victoria, British Columbia, Canada.

Yukon: Department of Travel and Information, Box 2703, Yukon, Canada.

The Department of Commerce in any town larger than a village in the North will provide a great deal of information on services in its own region.

Maps

Road maps and some others can be obtained from the sources listed on p. 149. For wilderness trips, backcountry travelers should obtain the best topographic maps available for the area in which they are interested. A free index of available maps covering Alaska can be obtained from the United States Geological Survey, Federal Center, Denver, Colorado 80225. Maps can then be ordered from the same source. For areas that are still inadequately mapped, aerial photographs or advance map proofs may be available. Write and ask about the status of mapping and photography to the Map Information Office, United States Geological Survey, Washington, D.C. 20242.

For Canadian index maps or specific quadrangles, write to the Map Distribution Office, Department of Mines and Technical Surveys, Ottawa, Ontario, Canada.

In overall trip planning, large scale maps are sometimes helpful. Some are listed in the indexes mentioned above, but wilderness visitors should also be aware of the World Aeronautical Charts, which are topographic maps on a scale of sixteen miles to the inch, available from the United States Department of Commerce, Coast and Geodetic Survey, Washington, D.C.

The Forest Service will provide maps of the two national forests in Alaska, though very little detail can be gotten from them. The service also has a number of handouts on specific trail systems, including reproductions of relevant sections of United States Geological Survey maps. Addresses are listed beginning on p. 153.

Ferries

Division of Marine Transportation
Pouch R
Juneau, Alaska 99801

British Columbia Ferries
816 Wharf Street
Victoria, British Columbia, Canada

Northland Navigation, Passenger Department
404 Hornby Street
Vancouver, British Columbia, Canada

Details of the ferry routes are discussed in chapter 2. Northland Navigation runs a steamer between Vancouver, Prince Rupert, and Stewart, British Columbia.

Trains

No railroad runs to the Yukon or Alaska, unfortunately. The Alaska Railroad, which runs from Anchorage to Fairbanks, past the entrance to McKinley Park, makes a worthwhile trip. One can be let off anywhere along the route by telling the conductor the mile number. The route is now paralleled by the new Anchorage-Fairbanks highway. The address is Alaska Railroad, Traffic Division, Box 7-2111, Anchorage, Alaska 99510.

A railroad connects the northern terminus of the Alaska Ferry System at Skagway with Whitehorse, capital of the Yukon. Cars are carried. The address is White Pass and Yukon Route, 1314 Joseph Vance Building, P.O. Box 2147, Seattle, Washington 98111.

A new railroad line is currently under construction north from Fort Saint James, British Columbia, to Dease Lake in the northern part of the province along the Coast Range Highway. This line passes through beautiful and otherwise inaccessible country, and it should provide unlimited opportunities for canoeists, kayakers, hikers, fishermen, and mountaineers. The line is intended mainly for mineral transportation. Write the British Columbia Railway, 1095 West Pender Street, Vancouver, British Columbia, Canada.

For rail service to the ferry system, one can take a train to Seattle or Vancouver, or go to Prince Rupert by Canadian National Railways, 1150 Station Street, Vancouver, British Columbia, Canada.

Buses

Coachways System, 15205 112th Avenue, Edmonton, Alberta, Canada, offers service to Prince George, Prince Rupert, Dawson Creek, Whitehorse, Dawson, and points along the Alaska Highway, with connections from Whitehorse to Fairbanks and Anchorage. Alaska Coachways, 11th & Cushman, Fairbanks, Alaska 99701, provides the connections and is the agent in Alaska.

Mount McKinley Bus Lines, 118 E. 6th Avenue, Anchorage, Alaska 99501, runs buses between Anchorage and Fairbanks, past McKinley Park, and also from Anchorage to Homer and Seward on the Kenai Peninsula.

Bus service within the Yukon from Whitehorse to Dawson, Ross River, and Faro is provided by the Norline Bus Company, 3rd Avenue, Whitehorse, Yukon, Canada.

Far West Bus Lines, Terrace Hotel, 4551 Grieg Avenue, Terrace, British Columbia, Canada, runs buses from Terrace to Stewart.

Westours Motor Coaches, 900 IBM Building, Seattle, Washington 98101, mainly runs tours, but they do have routes within Alaska that may be useful for the camper without his car, e.g., from Anchorage to Valdez.

Service from the terminus of the ferry system at Haines to Tok and Anchorage is provided by Alaska-Yukon Motor Coaches, 2434 32nd Avenue West, Seattle, Washington 98199. They also run buses between Fairbanks and Valdez.

Air Service

Scheduled air transportation is available to just about every community larger than a village in the North. Regular airline ticket agents can easily look up current schedules and connections. Recommendations on getting the best fares are discussed in chapter 3.

For private charters, lists of pilots for Alaska can be obtained from the division of tourism, listed on p. 149, or from the Alaska Travel Division. Local departments of commerce will also have listings of pilots in their areas.

The Department of Travel and Information, listed above, can provide a list of flying services within the Yukon Territory, as can the Department of Travel Industry in British Columbia.

Parks, National Forests, and Other Public Lands

Most land in the North, whether in the United States or Canada, is publicly owned. Even along roadways, where private ownership is naturally concentrated, most of the country is under the jurisdiction of one or another government agency. This is a boon to the camper and the outdoorsman, since there are usually minimal restrictions on hiking and camping.

Information, rules, and often maps can be obtained by contacting the appropriate agency.

In Alaska, most of the land area is still under the jurisdiction of the Bureau of Land Management, the main office of which in Alaska is at 555 Cordova, Anchorage, Alaska 99501. The Bureau of Land Management operates a number of campgrounds in Alaska, which are listed in appropriate sections of this book.

There are two national forests in Alaska, both situated along the southern and southeastern coast. *Chugach National Forest* includes a large part of the Kenai Peninsula, the coast and islands to the east of it, and Afognak Island, north of Kodiak Island. A map of Chugach National Forest and information on maintained trails can be obtained by writing Forest Supervisor, Chugach National Forest, Anchorage, Alaska 99501. This map also shows the location of Forest Service cabins mentioned a number of times in the text. The cabin designation on the map indicates to which ranger district one should write to reserve a particular cabin. The district addresses are Anchorage Ranger District, 6927 Seward Highway, Anchorage, Alaska 99501; Kenai Ranger District, P.O. Box 275, Seward, Alaska 99664; Ranger District, Chugach National Forest, P.O. Box 280, Cordova, Alaska 99574.

Tongass National Forest includes nearly all the area of the Alaska Panhandle, except for Glacier Bay National Monument. It is some of the most beautiful country in the world—vast forests, precipitous and glaciated peaks, pristine lakes, and fine rushing rivers. It also supports a great deal of wildlife. Because of the heavy rainfall in most of this region, Forest Service cabins make particularly good bases of operation for many, particularly family, campers. The forest is supervised in two units, and information on trails and cabins, together with a map of the forest, can be obtained from either: Supervisor, North Unit, Tongass National Forest, P.O. Box 1049, Juneau, Alaska 99801; or Supervisor, South Unit, Tongass National Forest, P.O. Box 2278, Ketchikan, Alaska 99901. As with Chugach, reservations for cabins must be made with district ranger offices and more detailed information can be obtained from them concerning their particular bailiwicks. They are: Chatham Ranger District, Juneau, Alaska 99801; Sitka Ranger District, Sitka, Alaska 99835; Petersburg Ranger District, Petersburg, Alaska 99833; Wrangell Ranger District, Wrangell, Alaska 99929; Craig Ranger District, Craig, Alaska 99921; Kasaan Ranger District, Ketchikan, Alaska 99901; and Ketchikan Ranger District, Ketchikan, Alaska 99901.

The national park system, though it has only a few areas in Alaska at this time, does have jurisdiction over three regions of great interest to campers: *McKinley National Park,* Glacier Bay National Monument, and *Katmai National Monument.* Information about all of them can be obtained by writing to the Public Information Office, National Park Service, 343 W. 6th Avenue, Anchorage, Alaska 99501. For more detailed information, write the supervisor of the particular unit: Mount McKinley National Park, P.O. Box 9, McKinley Park, Alaska 99755; Glacier Bay National Monument, P.O. Box 1089, Juneau, Alaska 99801; Katmai National Monument, P.O. Box 7, King Salmon, Alaska 99613.

Much less well known and less visited are the national wildlife refuges, administered by the Fish and Wildlife Service. There are currently eighteen refuges in Alaska, ranging in size from the great Arctic National Wildlife Range, with an area of almost nine million acres, to tiny forty-two-acre Hazy Islands. In general, the refuges are

Two Dall sheep, a ewe and a lamb, graze near the vegetation line in McKinley National Park.

wilderness, difficult of access, with no prepared campgrounds or other facilities. Visits to them can be very rewarding, particularly for those interested in viewing native wildlife. Kenai National Moose Range, a one and three quarter million-acre refuge on the Kenai Peninsula is accessible by road at certain points, and some campgrounds and trails are provided. Hunting and fishing are permitted in some of the national wildlife refuges. General information on the refuges can be obtained by writing the Area Supervisor, Alaska Wildlife Refuges, United States Fish and Wildlife Service, Anchorage, Alaska 99502. More detailed questions should be directed to the refuge manager at the address listed below for the particular preserve in which you are interested.

The *Arctic National Wildlife Range*, located in the northeast corner of Alaska, is perhaps the most important and interesting refuge in the country, presenting incomparable opportunities for observation of wildlife, backpacking, climbing, or simply communing with the wilderness. Flying in would normally be the only practicable way to get there. Write 1412 Airport Way, Fairbanks, Alaska 99701.

To the west and south along the coast of the Bering Sea are six refuges, some on the mainland coast and some on large or tiny islands out to sea. Many very important nesting areas for seabirds and waterfowl are found here, among the river deltas, sea cliffs, beaches, and tundra. There are also herds of musk oxen, reindeer, and other land mammals, as well as hair seals, sea lions, and walrus. Northernmost of these refuges is *Chamisso National Wildlife Refuge*, a small group of islands in Kotzebue Sound, north of the Seward Peninsula, a very important breeding area for a number of arctic seabirds. Farther south, on the Yukon River delta, is the northern part of *Clarence Rhode National Wildlife Range*, the southern part of which begins a hundred miles farther south on the coast, across from the million-acre island that comprises *Nunivak National Wildlife Refuge*. Nearby is *Hazen Bay National Wildlife Refuge*, consisting of Kigigak Island. Two hundred and fifty miles farther out to sea are the seabird rookery islands that constitute *Bering Sea National Wildlife Refuge*. Still farther south is *Cape Newenham National Wildlife Refuge*, which takes its name from the promontory at its western tip. Its 265,000 acres provide a huge nesting colony for seabirds, a major stopover for migrating waterfowl, and habitat for a number of marine mammals. All of this group of refuges are managed from a central office, and communications can be directed to Box 346, Bethel, Alaska 99559.

Along the great spine running first southeast and then due east from the main body of Alaska, separating the Pacific Ocean from the Bering Sea and forming the Alaska Peninsula and the Aleutian Islands and extending well over a thousand miles out to sea, are five more units of the national wildlife refuge system. South of the peninsula proper are several islands providing habitat for seabirds, sea lions, and sea otters and comprising *Semidi* and *Simeonof National Wildlife Refuges*. At the tip of the peninsula proper is 320,000-acre *Izembek National Wildlife Range*, with populations of caribou and brown bear and fantastic numbers of waterfowl. The western part of the Aleutian chain itself forms the *Aleutian Islands National Wildlife Refuge*. There are some caribou and brown bear, but most of the Aleutians are home for seabirds and marine mammals, including sea otters. Some tiny islands thirty miles north of the main Aleutian chain make up *Bogsolof National Wildlife Refuge*, which has many seabird and sea lion colonies. These reuges are all administered from Cold Bay, located near the tip of the Alaska Peninsula. The address is Pouch 2, Cold Bay, Alaska 99571. Anyone planning to visit the Aleutians should also inquire about whether military permission is required for the particular trip planned, since much of the Aleutian chain is under military jurisdiction.

Just west of the Alaska Peninsula is Kodiak Island, the western two-thirds of which constitutes *Kodiak National Wildlife Refuge*. The scenery on the island is spectacular, with rugged, forested mountains rising from the sea and wild streams carrying the fish that feed the island's large brown bear population. Since hunting is permitted, visitors should expect the bears to have a rather uncharitable view of humanity. Guide service may be required for visitors. Write Box 825, Kodiak, Alaska 99615.

Across Cook Inlet from the Kenai Peninsula is a high, rocky island, the summer home of vast numbers of gulls called black-legged kittiwakes, the *Tuxedni National Wildlife Refuge*. The refuge manager's address is Box 500, Kenai, Alaska 99611. The same address is used for the *Kenai*

National Moose Range, which occupies a large part of the Kenai Peninsula. Its one and three quarter million acres include much fine country for hiking, fishing, and camping.

The remaining three refuges are small islands in the Panhandle area of Alaska, which are maintained as seabird rookeries. *Saint Lazaria National Wildlife Refuge* is at the entrance of Sitka Sound; *Hazy Islands National Wildlife Refuge* is due south of Baranof Island where Sitka is located; and *Forrester Island National Wildlife Refuge* is at the southern tip of the Panhandle, on the seaward side of Ketchikan, and about eighty-five miles away. All these refuges are administered from the area office, Alaska Wildlife Refuges, 6917 Seward Highway, Anchorage, Alaska 99502.

Alaska state parks are listed at appropriate places in this book. Except for Chugach State Park, near Anchorage, and Denali State Park, south of McKinley on the Anchorage-Fairbanks highway, they are relatively small and are suitable mainly for car camping. The $10 annual permit for use can be obtained at the Tok Visitor Center by most campers. Those coming in by air can get the permits at auto licensing offices in most major Alaskan towns.

The only Canadian national park in the area covered by this book is the new *Kluane National Park,* Haines Junction, Yukon Territory, Canada. The area includes much of the Saint Elias Range, as well as the long-established Kluane Game Sanctuary. This area is a paradise for the experienced outdoorsman and lover of true wilderness.

More information on British Columbia's provincial parks can be obtained from the Department of Travel Industry, the address of which is listed at the beginning of this chapter. Nightly fees, where applicable, are collected at the provincial campgrounds. The more remote parks, such as Mount Edzia Provincial Park, near the Coast Range Highway, require difficult wilderness travel for access.

The $5 annual permit required for the use of the Yukon territorial campgrounds can be obtained from rangers or from tourist centers in towns along the Alcan.

Fishing

British Columbia: For information on regulations and licensing or to purchase a license, write the Fish and Wildlife Branch, Department of Recreation and Conservation, Parliament Buildings, 1019 Wharf Street, Victoria, British Columbia, Canada. Licenses may also be purchased at sporting goods stores.

Yukon Territory: Information and licenses may be obtained by writing the Department of Fisheries, Box 2703, Whitehorse, Yukon, Canada. Licenses may also be obtained at information centers and fishing stores.

Alaska: Licenses are widely available, but not until you get to the first town after entering the state. Information and regulations can be requested from the Alaska Department of Fish and Game, Sport Fish Division, Juneau, Alaska 99801; licenses from Department of Revenue, Fish and Game Licensing Section, Juneau, Alaska 99801.

Hunting

Unlike fishing, hunting is a pretty expensive sport for nonresidents anywhere in the North, at least if the hunter is interested in big game. Tag and trophy fees are high. Guides are required for nonresidents hunting big game in British Columbia and the Yukon. The same requirement exists in Alaska for nonresidents hunting sheep, brown bear, or grizzly. Regulations should be checked, since they change frequently. Current rules and licensing information can be obtained by writing the following addresses.

British Columbia: Same address as for fishing.

Yukon Territory: Director of Game, Box 2703, White-horse, Yukon, Canada.

Alaska: Department of Fish and Game, Juneau, Alaska 99801. Licenses: see listing under fishing.

Mountaineering

Climbers in Mount McKinley National Park must check in at park headquarters, and for any significant climbs, permission must be obtained in advance. It is advisable to begin correspondence at least six months ahead of time. Address the Superintendent, Mount McKinley National Park, P.O. Box 9, McKinley Park, Alaska 99755.

Thus far, there has been little regulation of climbing in Glacier Bay National Monument, but it would be prudent to write in advance before leaving on an expedition there: P.O. Box 1089, Juneau, Alaska 99613.

Other mountains in Alaska are mercifully unregulated, preserving every American's God-given right to do him or herself in in his or her own chosen way.

Mountains in the Yukon do require permission, but the regulation is considerably looser. Write to Mr. Craig P. Hughes, Alpine Advisory Committee, P.O. Box 2703, White-horse, Yukon, Canada. For mountains within the boundaries of the new Kluane National Park, write the park headquarters at Haines Junction, Yukon, Canada.

For both general information and specific routes, consult back issues of *Summit, Off Belay, Ascent, American Alpine Journal, Canadian Alpine Journal*, and *Mountain World.*

Guides

Guides for big game hunting are licensed by the state, territory, or province for particular areas. For a list of licensed guides in Alaska, write the Department of Commerce, Division of Occupational Licensing, State of Alaska, Pouch D, Juneau, Alaska 99801. For British Columbia and the Yukon, write to the addresses listed above under hunting.

A few guide services specializing in backpacking, kayaking, canoeing, float trips, and the like are springing up. The oldest is Camp Denali, Box D, College, Alaska 99701, for trips in McKinley National Park. Around Glacier Bay, try Alaska Discovery Enterprises, Box 41, Haines, Alaska. For float trips on the Yukon River, write Yukon River Tours, 1430 SW 85 Court, Miami, Florida 33144.

Those looking for guided trips on Mount McKinley itself should write Genet Expeditions, Talkeetna, Alaska 99676.

Index